Juli Bauer's
paleo cookbook

over 100 gluten-free recipes to help you shine from within

by Juli Bauer

photography by
Bill Staley and Hayley Mason

Shannon,
Enjoy every bite!
XOXO
Juli

Victory Belt Publishing Inc.

Las Vegas

First Published in 2015 by Victory Belt Publishing Inc.

ISBN-13: 978-1-628600-77-3

Photography: Bill Staley and Hayley Mason
Additional Photography: Andrea Flanagan
Design: Yordan Terziev and Boryana Yordanova

Printed in the U.S.A.
RRD 0115

thank you

To Hayley and Bill:

Words cannot express how grateful I am to have you two in my life. Without you both, my vision would never have been possible. Thank you for welcoming me into your home, for cooking me meals when I had no energy left, and for making this dream a reality. Your kindness and generosity will never be forgotten.

table of contents

acknowledgments

To any and every PaleOMG reader, this book wouldn't have been possible without you. You keep me excited to create new recipes, share new stories, and keep you laughing through the good times and bad.

To Brian, the guy who has believed in me from the beginning, man, I love you. Thank you for being there and loving me through every step of every cookbook. I truly cannot wait to marry you and see what really rad things we have in store.

To my mom and dad, thank you for your continued support and for letting me play dress-up with the jewelry from your store, Gene Bauer Goldsmith. This book wouldn't be nearly as girly without your beautiful gemstone flair.

To Stacy, my assistant and friend, who knew what our friendship had in store when we met years ago at a CrossFit gym? Thank you for your inspiration, your enthusiasm, and your excitement for improvement. I'm so lucky to have your part of my personal and business life.

To Victory Belt Publishing, you guys are seriously the best. Thank you for believing in me and helping me bring my vision to life. Your dedication to creating amazing books shows through with every author you take on. Thank you for letting me be part of that team.

foreword

It's impossible not to fall in love with Juli Bauer.

A few years ago, I was asked to present at a Paleo seminar way up in the Colorado Rockies—and as a rabid PaleOMG fan, there was no way I was going to pass up an opportunity to meet Juli in person. I knew she lived in Denver, so I asked our host to invite her to attend, not realizing that the seminar was over two hours from her home and accessible only via a circuitous route through the mountains. (Hey—geography's not my strong suit; before arriving in Colorado, I thought the Rocky Mountain State was somewhere in the Pacific Northwest. Near Seattle, maybe.)

Juli accepted without ever saying a word about the long trek. And despite getting lost in the mountains for a couple of hours, she arrived at the seminar with her famously gorgeous smile and sparkling personality. As soon as I spied Juli in the audience, I pulled her out of her seat to help me with a cooking demo. Without any hesitation, Juli happily complied—and even did a little dance for the audience. My presentation was a hit, due in large part to Juli's selflessness. By helping a Paleo sister out, Juli instantly and forever cemented her spot on my list of favorite people.

Meet Juli, and you'll be struck at her authenticity. She's just like her online persona: irreverent, sassy, fashion-forward, and food obsessed. She's your ideal best friend—if your BFF also happens to be a deliriously funny, super stylish *New York Times* bestselling cookbook author who can whip up a delicious Paleo-friendly meal on the spot—right after cheerfully coaching you through a brutal CrossFit WOD.

If you're a regular reader of PaleOMG like I am, you know all about Juli's infectious positivity and adventurous spirit. Over the years, we've cheered along with Juli every time she tackles a new role—cookbook author, puppy mom, and bride-to-be. But it's Juli's refreshing candor that draws us in day after day. We can all relate when she recounts awkwardly bumping into a two-timing ex-flame or vents about a popular activewear company changing her favorite workout pants. It doesn't hurt that she invariably offers a foolproof tasty recipe at the end of her daily posts. Her recipes aren't afterthoughts, though—and they always work perfectly.

I'm so excited about the new cookbook that you're holding in your hands. It perfectly encapsulates Juli and her strengths as a wildly successful blogger, home cook, and food personality: the food photos are drop-dead drool-worthy, the recipes are simple and flawless, and her wit and humor are woven throughout. I love checking in on Juli on the Internet, but I'm even happier to have her cookbook in my kitchen. Whenever I spy her beautiful cookbook on the counter, I'm reminded to goof off, cook great food, dress better, and practice my pull-ups. I know Juli will inspire the best in you, too!

—*Michelle Tam*, **New York Times**
bestselling author of *Nom Nom Paleo*

introduction

If you've just opened this book, I'm excited to inform you that all your hopes, dreams, and desires have come true. You have found yet another cookbook either to sit on your shelf collecting dust or to display proudly in your kitchen as you cook every single one of these recipes. There are two kinds of people out there: the ones who use cookbooks and the ones who collect cookbooks. I'm a collector, so there's no judgment here. Either way, every time you glance at this book you will see the face of a young woman who seems to be laughing at a chicken wing. *Why did I want to hold a chicken wing on the cover of my book, you may ask?* Because these chicken wings are freaking delicious, okay? Lay off! Oh, and because the stewed beef that I made was running off my fingers. Not my best look.

On a non-chicken-wing-related note, I'd love to tell you a little about myself. Mostly because that's what I do every.single.day. I blog. I blog about my life, my food, my kitchen, my dog, my now fiancé, my shoes, my skin, my waxing experience (yes, there was only one), my chocolate wasted nights, my alcohol wasted nights, my bargain shopping, and, oh, *did I mention my dog?* He's a pretty big deal in my household. Blogging is my day job. And cookbook creating is my side job. It's all quite fun.

But let's go way back. Back before blogs were invented and social media was created to ruin our lives. Back to the days when I figured out that I was obsessed with food. I always had friends growing up, *but my true best friend was Little Debbie.* Remember those snacks? The little plastic-wrapped treats of joy? Those were my best friends. I remember longing for lunch so that I could scrape the frosting out of the Swiss Rolls. Yeah, I said "longing." Who cares about learning when you have a sugar-packed treat waiting for you in your lunch box? Not me.

But then middle school and high school happened. The days of pure misery. No cool kids were obsessing over fake cream inside Swiss Rolls there. My high school experience was similar to the TV show *Glee*, but instead of getting a slushy thrown in my face, it was a Frosty that came plowing at me in a drive-by. Some hormone-crazed almost-a-woman legitimately threw a Frosty out a car window, aimed at my face. Yeah, high school wasn't my jam. But what I found much more insulting than the Frosty being whirled at me like a football was that *this girl had the audacity to throw out a full Frosty.* She just wasted it. Straight up. That may have been the moment I began to understand my unhealthy relationship with food.

Now, I'm not going to bore you with the non-fun part of life. Let's just say that I was like many girls growing up, feeling uncomfortable in my skin, being insecure 24/7. And the way I dealt with those insecurities was by starving myself at times, or binge eating, or counting calories, or working out for hours, or taking diet pills. Like many awkward teenagers, I was miserable. I hated what I saw in the mirror, and I hated that I never felt worthy of anything. I didn't believe in myself for about ten years. But that all sucks and is negative, so let's move on to the fun part: college.

College was just the best. A time of mistakes, self-discovery, finding gyros on a street corner at 2am and then debating about whether they are pronounced "YEE-ros" or "JI-ros" . . . oh, and Facebook. I did get an education, too. I received my bachelor's degree in health and exercise science. *Luckily, I always knew what interested me: food and working off my food.* But it wasn't my education that brought me to where I am today. It was CrossFit.

Let's just say that when I found CrossFit, it saved me. Not in the religious sort of way, but in the I'm-finally-not-miserable-and-I-finally-fit-in kind of way. I had spent ten years obsessing over every little thing that I saw wrong with myself instead of putting that energy toward something worthwhile. CrossFit gave me the opportunity to prove to myself that I am capable of great things. *CrossFit made me take responsibility for my own happiness for the first time in my life.*

But it was when I went to my first CrossFit competition that my views on health completely changed. Here were these women, of all different shapes and sizes, working their butts off for the same goal. It didn't matter what they looked like; it mattered how much heart they had and how hard they had trained. I had never been in a place where women respected other women. I grew up seeing women constantly trying to pull each other's hair out (literally) or ruin each other's lives behind their backs, and this was my first positive experience. That's when I knew I wanted to compete. I wanted to be around other inspiring women. I wanted to be part of a gym that wasn't about being the thinnest or about getting someone's phone number. *I wanted to be part of a gym that pushed health,* oozed inspiration, and showed other women that being strong and determined in the gym can lead to confidence and happiness in all aspects of life.

So that's what I did. I joined a CrossFit gym that made me feel empowered and excited about becoming the best me, and I began competing. Before I knew it, I had to face the facts: I was going to have to change the way I ate if I wanted to achieve my goal of competing in the CrossFit Regional. And let me explain something to you: I ate TERRIBLY. I liked—wait, no, I LOVED—Hot Pockets, animal crackers dipped in frosting, pizza, more pizza, cereal, and Oreos. *I loved anything that was packaged and easy to shove in my face in under 30 seconds.* I always believed that I could eat whatever I wanted if I worked out hard enough. But that wasn't the case for me, especially since I've had digestive issues my entire life. So I began researching and figuring out the truth: Diet really is important. The whole annoying "you are what you eat" bull crap is actually true, and I was hella pissed.

Let's get one thing straight: *The whole Paleo thing did not come overnight for me.* It wasn't like I woke up and said, "I'm going to remove all the things from my life that make me extremely happy," and then foraged the wilderness for my dinner. Um, no thank you. The process was extremely slow, one thing at a time. First I removed one slice of bread and had an open-faced sandwich. Over time I decided that I didn't need the other slice. Then I slowly stopped having my morning oats and tried smoothies, then transitioned into eating meat for breakfast. To me, it was a frightening process, so I had to take my time. Some people say that Paleo is easy, but that was *not* the case for me. It was very challenging and frustrating at times, but that was because I didn't know how to cook yet. So on Monday through Friday I ate boiled chicken, broccoli, and avocado for every meal, and then, once the weekend came, IT WAS ON. I would buy cookies and pizza and ice cream and eat until I was sick. It was like I had my life under control throughout the week, but I became an addict on the weekends. It had to stop. So I started researching recipes online.

At that point, there weren't many Paleo recipes or blogs out there. But there were a couple amazing ones, like health-bent.com and primalpalate.com, that really got me excited about cooking. I started following their recipes, crossing my fingers that the recipes would turn out. I made Paleo dinners, Paleo banana bread, Paleo pancakes, and Paleo biscuits. Any Paleo recipe I could find on the Internet that looked edible, I tried. But the thing was, I hated following recipes. I have a mad case of . . . let's just say multitasking (some professionals may call it ADHD), so my attention span is incredibly short. *I began making my own recipes* using techniques I found online and on cooking shows. I would try things that sometimes failed miserably and other times worked out perfectly.

Since I am naturally infatuated with food, I talked about it all.the.time. I told my friends, my parents, and the people I worked out with all about what I made at home. And I brought many of them snacks and treats to see what they thought. Surprisingly, they liked what I was sharing and told me that I should start a blog. I didn't understand what the hell a blog was. I mean, all I really cared about on the Internet at that time was Facebook. Ya know, my profile pic. But I found out that a blog included writing and sharing pictures, so I went for it and started up PaleOMG. AND I LOVED IT! Before I knew it, I was sharing multiple recipes each week along with a story about my life. I talked about how Paleo changed my life, about my love for food, about the workouts I was doing, about competing in CrossFit, about body issues, skin issues, boy issues. Everything that popped into my mind, I shared. And surprisingly, other people understood what I was going through. Even better, other people had experienced exactly what I had experienced, and that was incredibly comforting to me. *Who knew that so many people were as obsessed with food as I was?* If had known this in middle school, I would have had way more friends.

Let's skip ahead to the present day, where you'll find me writing cookbooks, creating new recipes to share on my blog, and finding happiness in my own little life. It's taken me 27 years to find a life and a "diet" that works for me. But thanks to CrossFit and the Paleo lifestyle, I have a life that makes me incredibly happy and fulfilled. *This life includes my Frenchie, fiancé, friends, fitness, and food.* All you need is F. Unless that F stands for Fake Food, because that's just not what I am into over here.

why I created this book

When I first started eating Paleo, I feared what I was going to miss out on. I didn't think that eating Paleo would change my life for the better; I just saw it as another bullshit diet that would make me miserable. I read blogs and books about Paleo that made me feel like if I didn't eat 100 percent Paleo 100 percent of the time, it wasn't worth doing at all. And that was incredibly disheartening. *I don't want you to feel that way.* I want you to know that sometimes Paleo may feel very difficult, and other times it will feel incredibly easy. I want you to know that just because you have a cupcake at your best friend's wedding doesn't mean that you are a failure. I want you to know that *you can do this.* Changing your diet is going to change your life. You can go all in or take it one step at a time, but either way, you can change your life for the better, starting with what you eat.

I created this book because Paleo truly has changed my life. It's made me healthier, happier, more energetic, and more in tune with my body. It's given me so much, and I want it to do the same for you. Do I sometimes eat gluten-free coffee cake at the bakeshop near my gym after a workout? Hell, yes, I do. Do I enjoy a cocktail out with my friends? Absolutely. That doesn't make me a bad person or a failure; it makes my life more balanced. Because of Paleo, I know what I can still enjoy without feeling sick and bloated afterwards. But it took me a little while to figure it out.

Through this cookbook, I hope to get you to the same point where I am: enjoying food and enjoying life at the same time. I hope to inspire you in the kitchen, to keep you from feeling like you're missing out, and *to keep you eating foods that help you shine from within.* We all deserve confidence and happiness, and through the Paleo diet and with some of my recipes, I know that you can get there.

why are people so obsessed with paleo right now?

Paleo is quite the fad right now. All the rage. But unlike other fad diets, this one can stick. Because it's based on what our ancestors ate and what our bodies were created to eat: simple, unprocessed foods that can be hunted or gathered. But since most of us don't hunt or gather (because DUH, we can order food on our smartphones), what we 21st-century people can do is search for the best-quality meats, plants, nuts, and seeds and BOOM, we're off to eating Paleo. It's simple. And everybody loves simple.

The best part about this Paleo "diet" is that it's not really a diet at all! It's an outline for how we should feed and take care of our bodies. Obviously, every body is a little different, so your specific outline is going to be different from someone else's. What I'm here to do is help guide you on your path to health through food by giving you alternatives to your beloved comfort foods and meals that make you feel full and satisfied. There is no perfect one-size-fits-all to anything—that's something you need to wrap your head around now. There's no magic pill or surgery that solves all issues. Everyone's health, body, and needs are different. Through my cookbook, *I hope you find some recipes that work for your body and become staples in your weekly rotation,* all while changing your health from the inside out.

You ready to try this "fad" that will actually turn into a lifestyle? You ready to change your life for the better? To feel better, live longer, and, let's face it, even look better? You're allowed to be vain. Eating healthier may seem daunting now, but once you get started, it's just going to snowball. You're going to get better at planning, better at cooking, and, before you know it, better at feeling good inside and out. And you know what? It won't be boring! You're going to love what you eat and how you feel, and you're going to shine in everything you do, all because of what you ate!

let's get your kitchen ready to go

cookware and tools

Keep in mind that I mix almost everything with a small spoon (like the kind you eat cereal with), not even a spatula. I like to keep things simple. And lick spoons along the way. But here are some tools that are helpful to have on hand for making the recipes in this book:

Sharp knives: Whatever kind suits you is fine, but I love my Moi Chef ceramic knives and my Wüsthof knives. Just don't cut your fingers off. I hear that hurts.

Measuring tools: Measuring isn't exactly fun, but it's definitely worth doing for most recipes, so don't skimp on the number of measuring cups and tools you keep in your house!

Cutting boards: I dig wood blocks.

Mixing bowls: The more, the better. I have both metal and plastic bowls. Metal helps keep foods cold while you mix them, such as my Whipped Cream on page 296.

Pots and pans: I don't care which ones you prefer; just find some pots and pans that work well for you. I recently bought my first Le Creuset cast-iron pot, and I'm obsessed with it. One of the best investments I've ever made. It just took me 27 years to save up for it. I also consistently use cast-iron skillets, and they have become my favorite pans to use for cooking.

Food processor and/or high-speed blender: You'll use it all the time and get your money's worth in no time flat, I promise you. I use a Blendtec, and it is perfect for making shakes, nut butters, and soups.

Immersion blender: Pureeing soups with an immersion blender is so much easier than trying to blend them in a regular blender.

Stand mixer: Welllll, I don't actually have one, but I wish I did, just for making buttercream (page 248). But since I just bought a Le Creuset pot, I need to save up for another ten years before buying a sweet KitchenAid. I still recommend one; it's awesome.

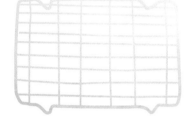

Baking sheets, rimmed and flat: This way, you can make a giant pizza crust (page 288). And a ton of other things, but who cares, PIZZA!

Wire racks: If you want foods to cool quickly or to cook evenly on all sides (like my chicken wings on page 82), you'll definitely want to have a few wire racks.

Glass baking dishes: An 8-inch square dish and a 9 x 13-inch dish will do ya well.

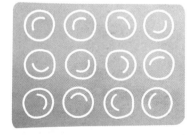

Muffin pans: Silicone muffin pans are the best. The muffins on page 38 will pop right out. It's amazing.

Slow cooker: You'll see me using a slow cooker in a few of my recipes, such as Baby Back Ribs (page 126) and Lechón Asado (page 138). You don't want to miss out, especially given how easy these recipes are!

food staples that you'll need for this book

Meat, poultry, eggs, and seafood: Includes beef, bison, lamb, pork, game meats, chicken, turkey, duck, eggs, fish, and seafood, including shellfish, organ meats, and high-quality cured meats. Read your labels! Look for: grass fed, grass finished, organic, locally sourced, pastured, natural, wild caught, free range, GMO free, and soy free. I know, that's a lot to think about, but over time it gets easier, and you will find the best stores and/or local farmers to buy from. If you have no stores near you, buying online in bulk is a great option.

Vegetables and fruits: Buy produce in season and organic. Purchasing at farmer's markets will keep you eating what is available around your area at that time. It will also keep you away from pesticide-laden vegetables and fruits. Ewwww. Nobody wants that.

Fats: Includes nuts and seeds, as well as these healthy fats and oils:

- Virgin coconut oil
- Extra-virgin olive oil
- Avocado oil
- Sesame oil
- Organic grass-fed butter (I usually use salted butter) and ghee
- Heavy cream (if you tolerate dairy)
- Bacon fat
- Lard
- Duck fat

Stick with raw nuts and seeds, as well as nut and seed butters (but not peanut butter—peanuts are legumes).

Fresh and dried herbs and spices: Make sure to use organic herbs and spices as often as possible.

Sweeteners

- Organic or raw honey
- Coconut sugar
- Pure maple syrup
- Maple sugar
- Blackstrap molasses
- Pitted Medjool dates
- Other dried fruits without added sugar
- Stevia extract

The fun extras

Flours

- Nut flours: almond, hazelnut, etc.
- Coconut flour
- Arrowroot flour/starch
- Tapioca flour/starch

Pops of flavor

- Bone broth: chicken, beef, turkey, etc. Not only does bone broth have a crap ton of nutrients in it, but it also tastes much more flavorful than the usual broth or stock. You can always make your own, but I like to use the Pacific Natural Foods brand of bone broth for quicker meals.
- Vegetable broth
- Coconut aminos
- Dijon mustard
- Vinegars
- Coconut butter
- Unsweetened coconut flakes and shredded coconut
- Canned full-fat coconut milk
- Unsweetened cocoa powder
- Pure vanilla extract
- Dark chocolate chips (I like Enjoy Life and Guittard brands)

get rid of these foods—you won't need them!

- **Grains:** wheat, barley, rice, corn, cereal, bread, oats, pasta, and quinoa
- **Legumes:** beans, peanuts, and lentils (anything that comes from a pod)
- **Soy**

- **Hydrogenated vegetable oils**
- **Refined sugar**
- **Processed/Packaged foods:** yes, that includes my bestie, Little Debbie

gray-area foods: dairy and white potatoes

The gray areas are so damn confusing when you start Paleo. One person will tell you that dairy is the devil, and the next person will be chugging a gallon of raw milk daily. Who to believe? What is fact and what is fiction? WHAT IS THE DAMN ANSWER? Calm down; I'm here to tell you that it's going to be okay.

Because everyone's body is different and we all have different genetics and backgrounds, the ways our bodies process food are going to be different as well. While someone will eat a piece of cheese and have an allergic reaction, other people can drink all the milk they want and not notice a difference. When you begin eating Paleo, I always recommend removing these gray-area foods and then adding them back into your diet after 30 days to see how your body is affected. If you feel no effects, then you may not have an issue with that food.

Dairy: Most important with dairy, if you can tolerate it, is to use high-quality, full-fat dairy. Raw milks and cheeses are best. You'll find me using goat cheese in a couple of the recipes in this book because it gives a pop of flavor, and many people who have issues with cow dairy don't have issues with goat dairy. Use the kind of dairy that works for your body or remove it altogether; my recipes will taste good with or without it!

White potatoes: Potatoes came back into style for Paleo recently. Someone said they were cool, and everyone got hella happy. Here's the thing about starches, though: If you are trying to lose weight, starches (such as tubers like white potatoes) are not always your best choice of carbohydrate, since we tend to overeat them and don't always burn them off through exercise. But if you are at your ideal weight and/or exercise on a regular basis, you may find that eating white potatoes keeps you thriving in and outside the gym! I generally eat sweet potatoes at home, but I'll chow down on a white potato whenever I see fit. Like when I get a craving for my Parsnip Potato Hash Browns on page 60.

food staples that I keep in my own kitchen

I keep these items on hand to keep me from diving headfirst into the cookie jar. And I have a French bulldog cookie jar, which is adorable, so holding back is hard work. But these simple foods make cooking easy, flavorful, and satisfying:

- Bacon
- Eggs
- Fine sea salt
- Garlic
- Grass-fed butter or ghee
- Homemade mayo (recipe on page 274)
- Nitrate-free chicken sausage
- Onions
- Skin-on chicken thighs
- Smoked salmon
- Sweet potatoes

These 11 simple ingredients pack a ton of flavor with a small amount of work. Individually, they can be used in all different ways: smoked salmon as a snack, scrambled eggs for breakfast, a baked sweet potato for a post-workout snack, bacon for breakfast, lunch, and dinner. And garlic and onions for the best flavor profile around. And if you put all these ingredients together, you actually have a crazy amazing hash. Hash can be eaten for breakfast, lunch, dinner, and yes, even a snack. This is exactly why I have these things on hand at all times. The more foods you have on hand that are easy to cook up, the less likely you will want to stop at a drive-thru on your way home from work. Remember, failing to plan is planning to fail. Don't you just hate how true that motivational quote is?!

And here are three more foods that I always like to have around . . . because they pretty much make a milkshake:

- Almond butter
- Almond milk
- Frozen bananas

Whenever I can't decide what I want to eat, or I have a mad case of a sweet tooth (which is 97 percent of the time) and don't feel like making my Layered Flourless Chocolate Cake (page 242), I blend these three things together and BOOM, I have a milkshake. And a milkshake is good no matter what the season or time of day and no matter what your age. Just a fact.

snacking makes everything better

The number-one question I get asked is what to snack on when starting Paleo. Here in America, we love snacking. There are grocery store snack aisles, fast food restaurants offering snack items, and vending machines. Snack foods are lurking around every corner; we are even raised with snack times built into our days. I still remember eating little snack-sized apple pies from McDonald's growing up. Excuse me while I gag a little.

When eating Paleo, you have to think through your snacks a bit more than you used to. But that's okay; using your brain is a good thing. What seems to work best for me is having a snack with protein first and fat second. I like snacks such as smoked salmon and almonds or sliced chicken and avocado. It doesn't have to be protein and fat, but those two things fill me up the fastest and keep me full the longest.

Honestly, when you start seeing all the options out there, snack combinations are endless. So I'm going to lay them all out for you. Okay, well, not all of them, because that list would go on forever, but I'll share my favorites! That way you can build your own snacks in no time flat using protein, fat, carbohydrate, and even a sexy spread to make it more thrilling. Yes, snacks should be thrilling.

Start with a protein:

- Smoked salmon
- Sliced turkey (nitrate and sugar free)
- Sliced ham (nitrate and sugar free)
- Sliced prosciutto
- Diced cooked chicken
- Chicken sausage (nitrate and sugar free)
- Leftover steak cut into chunks
- Hard-boiled eggs

Throw in a little fat:

- Avocado or guacamole
- Nuts: almonds, cashews, pistachios, walnuts, etc.
- Bacon

Yes, carbs, too!

- Fresh fruit, such as sliced apple, sliced pear, or a mandarin orange
- Dried fruit: raisins, figs, pitted dates
- Raw veggies, such as celery, carrots, cucumber, or shredded cabbage
- My favorite roasted veggies: broccoli, cauliflower, etc.
- Plantain chips

And you'll need a little Sexy Spread:

- Super Simple Mayonnaise (page 274)
- Dairy-Free Pesto (page 280)
- Hot sauce
- Balsamic vinegar

Here are some mix-and-match ideas that I eat on the reg:

- Sliced apples and almond butter
- Celery and almond butter with raisins
- Chicken, avocado, and hot sauce
- Almond butter stuffed in dates, wrapped in prosciutto
- Sliced pears wrapped in prosciutto, topped with balsamic vinegar
- Plantain chips with guacamole and chicken sausage
- Diced chicken mixed with mayo and pesto, on top of plantain chips
- Bacon Buffalo Deviled Eggs (page 206)
- Strips of cucumber wrapped around mayo and smoked salmon
- Leftover steak mixed with shredded cabbage and mayo

step into my kitchen

Let's just get it out there. Let's talk about the elephant in the room: I'm not a trained chef. No way, no how. I'm just a food-obsessed woman who is constantly looking for people to share that obsession with. That's the whole reason I taught myself how to cook and began blogging. I don't know how to make duck confit (even though it's one of my favorite things ever, and I need to learn right now because now I'm craving it) or how to debone a fish, but I love learning and trying new things. Why am I telling you this? Because if I can do it, ANYBODY can do it! I didn't know what the hell I was doing at first, but over time, as I cooked for myself more and more, recipes started tasting better and cooking became easier and more enjoyable.

Since I am no trained chef, you won't find me talking about air temperature control or giving ingredients in exact grams. I don't know about all that crap. But you won't need it, I promise you. I've made these recipes at different houses, at different times of the year, and at different altitudes, and they come out great every single time. Not sure of a sweet potato size for my Breakfast Baked Sweet Potatoes (page 58)? I swear, any size will work. I wouldn't lead you in the wrong direction—we're besties! Right? RIGHT?!

In the end, if you dropped by my kitchen, you would see that I'm a pretty simple cook. And messy, but that's besides the point. I like using the ingredients that taste best to me and are pretty easy to find. With these simple ingredients, you can make a recipe in a million different ways. Cooking is all about finding what tastes good to you and putting your own spin on a recipe every time you make it. Here are some tips that I've learned along the way:

Season your food well.

Even if you have no spices or herbs on hand, always use salt. Salt brings out the flavor in your food. And flavor is boss.

Take your time.

When I first began cooking, I would get my pan way too hot and end up burning the garlic and onion or whatever the hell else I was cooking. You don't want that. Burned is no good. Unless you are trying to sear something, take your time with your food and you'll get more flavorful, delicious meals.

Figure out the extra steps that make your meals come alive, and do those things consistently.

These three techniques keep my meals tasty and have people wondering why my food tastes so good:

Reducing: Want a sauce or soup to thicken up? Turn the heat down low and let it go. It will thicken up and the flavor will pop. I do this with my Sticky Sesame Teriyaki Chicken Wings on page 82.

Roasting peppers: This extra step is sooo worth it. If you can find green chiles in season, roasting them yourself before adding them to my Green Chile Hollandaise on page 74 will make a huge difference when it comes to flavor.

Braising and slow cooking: "Good things come to those who wait." They ain't lying about that.

my rules to paleo

It's my cookbook, and I can make my own rules if I want to. Also cry if I want to, mostly over Nicholas Sparks novels.

Failing to plan is planning to fail. I hate to get all deep here, but it must be said. If you come home absolutely starving and don't have food ready to cook or reheat, you will go off the deep end and stuff your face with whatever is near you. Chocolate, potato chips, dog food, anything. So plan ahead. Get your recipes done with early. Plan for your success by making a couple freezer meals and portable snacks for the week on Sunday so that you have food on hand for those desperate moments. Boom.

Do not eat with your mouth open. No one wants to hear you mashing your animal carcass. It's the 21st century, people. And don't make the joke that you're a eating like a caveman, so you'll act like one, too. I've heard that joke one too many times.

Just because caveman licked his fingers doesn't mean you have to. That's why we have water, soap, and napkins. Even if you washed your hands, you probably picked up some H1N1 virus or bird flu on the way to the dinner table. So keep your finger licking to your own house, by yourself, licking your own gross germs.

Don't just flat-out tell people that you eat Paleo because they are serving you a sandwich. It's like you're yelling at them. And then people feel like you're judging them for not eating Paleo. Just eat what you want, or remove the meat from the sandwich and eat it separately. If people question why you are dissecting your sandwich, tell them that you have a gluten allergy. Or tell them that you have IBS. That makes everyone uncomfortable, and they'll abandon the subject immediately.

Just because you're eating a Paleo dessert doesn't mean that it doesn't have calories in it. Believe me, *I'm not a fan of calories, but that doesn't mean they don't exist.* And dessert is still dessert. If you go eating all of my peanut butter pie in one sitting, not only will you feel awful, but your Lululemon spandex won't even fit anymore. You're talking to the queen of dessert experimentation here. Just take my word for it.

Do not say, "Well, I already ate one cookie and ruined my diet, so I might as well each crap for the rest of the day." That's the dumbest thing I've ever heard. Do you ever hear people say, "I already got in one car accident today, so I might as well do it again"? No. Because that is stupid. Don't be stupid. We all have our bumps in the road. They won't ruin everything you've worked for. Get back to eating your delicious planned-out dinner and feel great about life. *This way of eating isn't supposed to make you feel like a failure, so don't let it.*

tips to make paleo easier

Like I said, switching to the Paleo lifestyle took some time for me, and it wasn't always easy. If you're just starting out, here are some tips to help with your transition:

Keep meat and veggies in the freezer for the end of the week when your fridge is empty and you need a quick meal.

I try to keep my freezer stocked with ground beef, chicken breasts, and salmon since I know that those proteins are easy to cook up in a pinch. Grabbing a few bags of frozen veggies such as broccoli, cauliflower, and green beans makes for easy pan cooking or oven roasting when you're out of the fresh kind.

Buy in bulk and online.

The Internet is full of deals when it comes to food—utilize them! Amazon and Thrive Market are great online tools for finding the ingredients you need.

Double your recipes for leftovers.

You'll never regret having leftovers for lunch the next day.

Make food ahead of time.

Even though that is a no-brainer, having food ready to heat up on the busy days that leave you starving will help keep you on track. Try my casseroles on pages 80 and 94 for delicious leftovers.

Stop complaining that Paleo is expensive.

No duh, it's expensive. Being healthy is expensive. But if you are that worried about it, you may need to reprioritize your spending. Remember, being healthy now will help keep your medical bills in check later in life. Okay, I'll get off my soapbox now.

Honestly, the only way to make Paleo easier is to get cooking! The more you cook, the better you'll get at it, and the more you'll enjoy it. So let's do it! Let's get cooking so that you can enjoy the delicious taste of gluten- and grain-free eating and the amazing health benefits of the Paleo diet. I promise you, you're going to love every bite of it!

breakfast

The early bird gets the worm . . . or donut.

I grew up loving cereal. Because it's the greatest thing ever. To have pure sugar enter your mouth at 7 in the morning before school is amazing. And insane. No wonder kids are exhausted by 9am—they're all coming off a sugar high! And my cereal addiction didn't end at grade school; nope, it went all the way into college. My dorm cafeteria had about 20 different cereals "on tap." It was fantastic. I would have my overflowing bowl of cereal with a sugar-flooded chai. Best breakfast, lunch, and dinner ever? Duh. *Along with my Freshman 15.*

You know the funny part of all this (other than my Freshman 15)? I had Loren Cordain as a professor. The author of *The Paleo Diet*. He taught us all about what is Paleo, why Paleo, this and that Paleo. But I was a freshman in college, and *when confronted with 20 shades of cereal, I gave in quickly.* If Loren Cordain had just explained to me that I could still have Paleo waffles and muffins on this so-called "Paleo diet," I would have tossed the cereal years earlier. But Paleo waffles aren't really his style. It's cool, Loren; you were shaping my squishy little freshman brain without either of us knowing it. Pretty rad.

dirty chai
chocolate muffins

Yield: 1 dozen muffins

Prep time: 10 minutes, plus time to make the almond milk

Cook time: 25 minutes

I have a bazillion muffin recipes on my blog, from apple cinnamon to chocolate chip to even "peanut butter" and jelly stuffed muffins. I just love them. Want to know an even more exciting fun fact? One of the first Paleo recipes I created on my own was a recipe for blueberry chai muffins. Not as exciting as you had hoped? Damn.

½ cup coconut flour

½ cup tapioca flour/starch

½ cup unsweetened cocoa powder

½ cup coconut sugar

1 teaspoon instant coffee

contents of 1 chai tea bag

½ teaspoon baking soda

½ teaspoon baking powder

pinch of fine sea salt

4 large eggs, room temperature

½ cup melted coconut oil

½ cup Sweet Almond Milk (page 254)

½ cup cold brew coffee (or brewed coffee that has been chilled)

½ cup dark chocolate chips

1. Preheat the oven to 350°F. Line a muffin tin with paper liners, or use a silicone muffin pan or silicone baking cups.

2. In a large bowl, whisk together the flours, cocoa powder, coconut sugar, instant coffee, chai tea spices, baking soda, baking powder, and salt.

3. In a medium bowl, whisk together the eggs, coconut oil, almond milk, and brewed coffee. Pour the wet ingredients into the dry ingredients and mix well. Fold in the chocolate chips.

4. Use an ice cream scoop to scoop the mixture into the lined muffin cups or silicone cups. Bake for 25 minutes or until a toothpick inserted into the middle of a muffin comes out clean.

5. Store any leftover muffins in a closed container in the refrigerator for up to 1 week.

You may also like:

Mini Chocolate Hazelnut Scones (page 44)

Chocolate Hazelnut Pumpkin Bread (page 46)

Sweet Potato Waffles (page 54)

coconut lavender pistachio
mini donuts

Yield: 14 or 15 mini donuts

Prep time: 10 minutes, plus time to make the almond milk

Cook time: 15 to 20 minutes

● ● ● ●

I grew up on donuts. Truly. Every weekend involved at least one donut. I remember going to Winchell's Donuts as a child and always getting this giant, crispy-yet-soft coffee cake donut. It was unbelievably good. No, seriously, un.freaking.believable. And when Winchell's wasn't close by, we would grab donuts from the grocery store. I would even have a dozen on hand at my swim meets to eat between races. For real. I would swim to be healthy, then backtrack right to my donuts. *I'm almost positive that I punched my mother when I was three years old when she said I couldn't have a donut.* It's pretty obvious what my first addiction was.

for the donuts:

4 large eggs, room temperature

½ cup melted coconut oil

½ cup Sweet Almond Milk (page 254)

½ cup maple syrup

1 teaspoon vanilla extract

½ cup coconut flour

¼ cup tapioca flour/starch

½ teaspoon baking soda

pinch of fine sea salt

1 tablespoon lavender buds, finely chopped

for the frosting:

3 tablespoons honey

3 tablespoons melted coconut butter

2 tablespoons butter, ghee, or coconut oil

1 teaspoon vanilla extract

for garnish:

¼ cup raw pistachio meats, crushed

1 teaspoon lavender buds, finely chopped

1 Heat up a mini donut maker.

2 In a small bowl, whisk together the eggs, coconut oil, almond milk, maple syrup, and vanilla extract.

3 Sift the coconut flour into a large bowl, then add the tapioca flour, baking soda, salt, and lavender buds and whisk to combine. Pour the wet mixture into the dry mixture and mix until smooth.

4 Transfer the batter to a pastry bag or gallon-size resealable plastic bag with one corner cut off. Squeeze about 2 to 3 tablespoons of the batter into each well of the donut maker.

5 Cook for 5 to 7 minutes, until the donuts are browned. Set aside on a wire rack to cool and repeat until the batter is gone.

6 Make the frosting: Combine all the frosting ingredients in a small saucepan over medium heat. Cook, stirring, until melted and soft, about 3 minutes.

7 Place the frosting in a shallow bowl. Dunk the top of each donut in the frosting, then sprinkle with the pistachios and lavender buds.

8 Store any leftover donuts in a closed container in the refrigerator for up to 1½ weeks.

mini chocolate
hazelnut scones

Yield: 16 mini scones

Prep time: 10 minutes, plus time to make the hazelnut spread

Cook time: 20 minutes

● ● ● ●

Everything is cuter when it's mini sized. And then it's better portion control . . . sometimes.

1½ cups hazelnut flour

½ cup coconut sugar

⅓ cup unsweetened cocoa powder

¼ cup tapioca flour/starch

½ teaspoon baking powder

pinch of fine sea salt

½ cup melted coconut oil

1 large egg, room temperature

1 teaspoon vanilla extract

⅓ cup dark chocolate chips

¼ cup Easy Chocolate Hazelnut Spread (page 292)

1. Preheat the oven to 350°F. Line a baking sheet with parchment paper.

2. In a large bowl, whisk together the hazelnut flour, coconut sugar, cocoa powder, tapioca flour, baking powder, and salt.

3. In a small bowl, whisk together the coconut oil, egg, and vanilla extract. Pour the wet ingredients into the dry ingredients and mix together. Fold in the chocolate chips.

4. Place the dough on a sheet of parchment paper and form it into a rectangle about ½ inch thick. Cut the rectangle in half, then cut the 2 rectangles in half once more, creating 4 strips. Cut each strip in half widthwise, then cut each square on the diagonal, creating 2 mini scones per square, 16 mini scones total. Use a spatula to pick up the scones and arrange them on the lined baking sheet, spaced about 1 inch apart.

5. Bake for 20 minutes or until set. Let cool on the pan for 5 minutes, then use a spoon to drizzle the hazelnut spread on top.

6. Store any leftover scones in a closed container in the refrigerator for up to 1 week.

Other ways to use hazelnuts and chocolate:

Chocolate Hazelnut Pumpkin Bread (page 46)

Chocolate Hazelnut Iced Mochas (page 256)

Easy Chocolate Hazelnut Spread (page 292)

chocolate hazelnut
pumpkin bread

Yield: One 9 by 5-inch loaf (8 slices)

Prep time: 5 minutes, plus time to make the hazelnut spread

Cook time: 1 hour

My mom couldn't get me to eat much of anything healthy while I was growing up. Hence I ate Little Debbie snacks all the time. But I do remember her buying this pumpkin loaf from the grocery store that I would eat until I felt sick. It was super dense, really moist (sorry for using that word), and so flavorful. *It was probably the healthiest thing I ate at that point in my life.* Thank goodness my taste buds changed over time.

1 tablespoon butter, ghee, or coconut oil, for greasing the pan

1 cup almond butter or other nut or seed butter of choice

½ cup pumpkin puree

1 medium banana, mashed

¼ cup honey

2 large eggs, room temperature

1 tablespoon pumpkin pie spice

3 tablespoons coconut flour

½ teaspoon baking soda

½ teaspoon baking powder

pinch of fine sea salt

¾ cup Easy Chocolate Hazelnut Spread (page 292)

toasted hazelnuts, for garnish

1. Preheat the oven to 350°F. Grease a 9 by 5-inch loaf pan with butter. For easy cleanup and to help you remove the bread from the pan, cut a piece of parchment paper to fit the length of the pan with parchment hanging over the sides.

2. Place the almond butter, pumpkin puree, banana, honey, eggs, pumpkin pie spice, coconut flour, baking soda, baking powder, and salt in a food processor and puree until smooth. Wipe down the sides of the food processor if needed and puree once more.

3. Pour the batter into the prepared loaf pan and smooth out the top. Use a spoon to push down the middle, pressing the batter up the sides of the pan and creating a well for the hazelnut spread.

4. Melt the hazelnut spread in a double boiler or in a bowl in the microwave. Pour the melted hazelnut spread into the well in the batter.

5. Bake for 1 hour or until a toothpick inserted into the center of the loaf comes out clean. Let cool in the pan for 10 minutes before removing from the pan, slicing, and garnishing with toasted hazelnuts.

6. Store the bread in a closed container in the refrigerator for up to 1½ weeks.

the fluffiest
mini cinnamon pancakes

Yield: Twenty to twenty-two 2-inch pancakes

Prep time: 5 minutes, plus time to make the almond milk

Cook time: 20 to 30 minutes

½ cup coconut flour

½ cup tapioca flour/starch

½ teaspoon baking powder

½ teaspoon baking soda

1 teaspoon ground cinnamon

pinch of fine sea salt

3 large eggs, room temperature

¾ cup Sweet Almond Milk (page 254)

1 tablespoon honey

1 teaspoon vanilla extract

1 to 2 tablespoons ghee, butter, or coconut oil, for greasing the pan

maple syrup, for serving

You know the kids' movie *Despicable Me*? With Steve Carell as the angry upside-down-triangle–shaped dad and the adorable little girls? Man, I love that movie. I love Steve Carell even more. But the part of that movie that sticks in my head is when one of the little girls gets a giant stuffed animal from a fair and screams, *"It's so fluffyyyyy!"* That's what these pancakes are like.

① In a large bowl, whisk together the flours, baking powder, baking soda, cinnamon, and salt.

② In a medium bowl, whisk together the eggs, almond milk, honey, and vanilla extract. Pour the wet mixture into the dry mixture and mix until smooth.

③ Grease a large sauté pan or griddle pan with ghee and place it over medium heat. Using a 1½-tablespoon cookie scoop, pour the batter onto the pan, cooking three or four 2-inch pancakes at a time. Cook for 2 to 3 minutes, until bubbles begin to form in the batter, then flip and cook for another 2 to 3 minutes, until the pancakes are fluffy and cooked through in the center. Remove from the pan and set aside, then repeat with the remaining batter.

④ Serve the pancakes topped with maple syrup. Store leftovers in the refrigerator for up to 2 days or in the freezer for up to 1 week, and thaw them before reheating in a pan.

Use these pancakes for:

Mini Cinnamon Pancake Bake (page 50)

Tip:
If the batter seems too thick, add more almond milk. Different brands of tapioca and coconut flour seem to act a little differently, so it may need a bit more liquid.

French toast is amazing. Stuffed French toast is even better. But baked French toast wins it all. Because it's so damn easy. All you have to do is make some mini pancakes, line them up like a bunch of second graders on a field trip,

whisk some liquid, and pour it all together to bake. Boom, you have a French toast bake that takes it to a whole new level using pancakes. Your weekend brunch plans will never be the same.

mini cinnamon
pancake bake

Serves: 4

Prep time: 5 minutes, plus time to make the pancakes

Cook time: 40 to 45 minutes

● ● ● ●

I always envy people who make those overnight French toast bakes with thick, crispy bread, because they look like the best thing ever to cross this earth. Truly. So I made this—no bread needed. Just these adorable little pancakes baked all together in a *happy little house.*

1 tablespoon coconut oil, butter, or ghee, for greasing the pan

1 batch Mini Cinnamon Pancakes (page 48)

1 cup full-fat coconut milk

3 large eggs, room temperature

1 tablespoon vanilla extract

½ teaspoon ground cinnamon

for the topping:

¼ cup (½ stick) butter, softened

2 tablespoons granulated maple sugar

¼ teaspoon ground cinnamon

maple syrup, for serving

1. Grease a small baking dish (such as an 8-inch square baking dish or a 9 by 5-inch loaf pan) with coconut oil. Layer the pancakes in rows.

2. Preheat the oven to 350°F.

3. Whisk together the coconut milk, eggs, vanilla extract, and cinnamon. Pour the mixture over the pancakes, then press the pancakes down into the mixture to help them soak up the liquid.

4. Bake for 40 to 45 minutes, until the egg mixture has completely set in the middle and is no longer jiggly.

5. While the pancake mixture is baking, make the topping. In a small bowl, mix together the butter, maple sugar, and cinnamon.

6. Use a knife or spoon to spread the topping mixture on top of the pancake bake. If it is still rather warm, the topping mixture will melt. If it doesn't, place the pan back in the oven for 2 to 3 minutes, until the topping mixture has melted.

7. Serve drizzled with maple syrup.

Tasty tips:

● Add fruit between the pancakes for a fruity surprise when you bite in.

● Add nuts or chocolate chips for another texture and flavor element.

sweet potato
waffles

Yield: Four 6-inch waffles

Prep time: 10 minutes

Cook time: 1 hour

● ● ● ●

1 small white sweet potato or
1 cup mashed white sweet potato

3 large eggs, room temperature, whisked

3 tablespoons maple syrup, plus extra for serving

1 teaspoon vanilla extract

2 tablespoons butter, melted, plus extra butter for serving

1 cup blanched almond flour

⅓ cup tapioca flour/starch

½ teaspoon baking soda

½ teaspoon baking powder

¼ teaspoon ground cinnamon

Tasty tip:
A dollop of whipped cream (page 296) would be super decadent for a weekend brunch treat.

I made these waffles with sweet potatoes, keeping in mind those people who work out early in the morning and need a quick and filling breakfast. I coach some mornings at my CrossFit gym, and my 6am crew are some of the hardest-working people I know. But they are also the people who forget to eat breakfast because they are thinking about their work. Type-A weirdos. Sweet potatoes are an amazing post-workout snack, and you can keep these waffles in the freezer to thaw and toast for a quick and easy breakfast. *My 6am Type-A weirdo crew will never have an excuse for not eating a great breakfast again!*

1 Preheat the oven to 425°F. Wrap the sweet potato in foil and bake for 35 to 40 minutes, until soft.

2 Let the sweet potato cool to the touch, then peel off the skin, place the flesh in a large bowl, and mash with a fork until smooth.

3 Mix in the eggs, maple syrup, vanilla extract, and butter and whisk until smooth.

4 Add the flours, baking soda, baking powder, and cinnamon and mix well.

5 Heat up a waffle iron and ladle about ⅓ cup of the batter into the iron. Cook until crispy on the outside; the cooking time will vary depending on your waffle iron. Set aside and repeat with the remaining batter.

6 Serve with butter and maple syrup.

7 Store any leftover waffles in a closed container in the refrigerator for up to 1 week, or freeze for later. Defrost and toast before serving.

Variation: Chocolate Waffles

For chocolate waffles, add 3 tablespoons of unsweetened cocoa powder to the other dry ingredients in step 4.

blueberry vanilla
chia pudding parfaits

Yield: 2 large parfaits

Prep time: 5 minutes, plus time to make the almond milk and whipped cream and at least 3 hours to refrigerate

● ● ● ●

This parfait screams breakfast bar, dontchathink? I would never be fancy enough to create a breakfast bar, but if I did, it would definitely include all the ingredients to make this recipe. The best part is that this parfait makes an amazing snack, too.

½ cup Sweet Almond Milk (page 254)

½ cup full-fat coconut milk

1 heaping tablespoon almond butter or other nut or seed butter of choice

1 teaspoon vanilla extract

2 tablespoons honey*

¼ cup chia seeds

1 batch Whipped Cream (page 296)

1 cup fresh blueberries

¼ cup raw walnuts, roughly chopped

1. Place the milks, almond butter, vanilla extract, and honey in a blender and blend until smooth.

2. Place the blended mixture in a large resealable jar (or two smaller jars), then add the chia seeds. Seal the jar, shake, and refrigerate for at least 3 hours or overnight. I like to let the chia seed mixture sit in the refrigerator for 1 hour, then shake it up once more to make sure that the chia seeds and liquids don't separate.

3. Once the chia seeds have developed a pudding-like texture, make the whipped cream.

4. In 2 jars, bowls, or parfait glasses, layer the chia pudding, blueberries, and whipped cream and top with walnuts.

* Replace the honey with 1 dropper of stevia extract for a sugar-free option.

Check out more light breakfast options:

Prosciutto Herb Frittata (page 68)

Apple Fennel Breakfast Sausage (page 62)

Breakfast Tacos (page 70)

breakfast baked
sweet potatoes

Serves: 2 to 4

Prep time: 15 minutes

Cook time: 1½ hours

● ● ● ●

2 sweet potatoes or yams

3 slices bacon

¼ pound breakfast sausage or ground pork (breakfast sausage will have more flavor)

6 large eggs, divided

1 tablespoon chopped fresh chives

½ teaspoon fine sea salt

¼ teaspoon cayenne pepper

Tasty tip:
Here's a brunch appetizer idea: Slice the baked sweet potatoes and put a toothpick through each slice!

I love when my entire meal is packed into one bite. It's the reason why people are so addicted to breakfast sandwiches: They want more food with less work. That's this, minus the crap ingredients. Hooray!

1. Preheat the oven to 425°F.

2. Wrap each sweet potato in foil and place on a baking sheet. Bake for 40 to 45 minutes, until soft to the touch. Then turn the oven temperature down to 325°F.

3. Set the sweet potatoes aside until they are cool enough to handle. While they cool, cook the bacon in a medium sauté pan over medium heat until crispy, about 10 minutes, then set aside to cool. Remove the excess bacon fat from the pan, add the sausage, and cook until no longer pink, about 10 minutes. Once the bacon is cool, chop it into small pieces.

4. In a medium bowl, whisk 4 eggs, then mix in the sausage, bacon, chives, salt, and cayenne pepper, reserving some bacon and chives for garnish.

5. Carefully cut off the top third of each baked sweet potato, then use a spoon to hollow it out, leaving about ¼ inch all around to make sure that nothing will seep through.

6. Place the sweet potatoes on the baking sheet and fill each one with half of the egg mixture. Bake for 20 to 25 minutes, until the eggs no longer jiggle in the middle.

7. For aesthetic appeal and more protein, scramble the 2 remaining eggs and use for garnish, along with the reserved bacon and chives.

parsnip potato
hash browns

Yield: Eight 3- to 4- inch patties
(serving 4)

Prep time: 10 minutes

Cook time: 20 to 25 minutes

Sometimes a simple breakfast is the best breakfast. These crispy hash browns take me back to the days when I used to end up at Waffle House at 2 in the morning to eat a plateful of cheesy, eggy, crispy hash browns in hopes of ridding myself of a hangover the next morning. It usually worked. Oh, college, you crazy bastard. *This is the lightened-up version that won't send you into a tailspin of "what am I doing with my life?" questions.*

3 medium parsnips

1 large russet potato

fine sea salt

¼ to ½ cup coconut oil, ghee, or butter

finely chopped fresh chives, for garnish

Tasty tips:

- Be patient with these suckers. If you try to cook them too fast on super high heat, they'll burn and taste terrible. Patience is key here. You want them to taste crispy without the char.

- Serve with eggs and bacon, some breakfast sausage (page 62), or even a slice of frittata (page 68).

1. Peel the parsnips and potato, then finely shred them into a large bowl. Sprinkle with salt and mix to combine.

2. In a large sauté pan over medium-high heat, warm ¼ cup of coconut oil until shimmering but not smoking. While the oil is heating, use an ice cream scoop to scoop up a portion of the parsnip mixture, use your hands to squeeze out the excess liquid, then flatten into a patty. Repeat with the remaining mixture; it will make about eight 3- to 4-inch patties.

3. Place 3 or 4 patties in the hot oil (being sure not to crowd the pan to keep the oil hot) and sprinkle with a bit more salt. Fry for about 5 to 6 minutes, until golden brown, sticking together, and ready to flip. Turn over and cook for 3 to 4 minutes or until golden brown on the bottom. Remove with a spatula and place on a paper towel to soak up the excess oil.

4. Repeat with the remaining patties. You may need to add more oil to the pan as they cook. Keep the pan well oiled so the hash browns don't stick to the pan.

5. Serve garnished with fresh chives.

Spicy Sweet Potatoes (page 186)

Pulled Pork Benedict with Green Chile Hollandaise (page 74)

You may also like:

apple fennel
breakfast sausage

Yield: Eight 2-inch patties (serving 4)

Prep time: 10 minutes

Cook time: 25 minutes

Breakfast sausage is one of those things that is super hard to find without a ton of added crap. Not to worry, my friend: Now you have this recipe that you can make into patties, cook, and add to a frittata (page 68), *or even make into breakfast meatballs.* Yep, I've done that on my blog.

2 teaspoons fennel seeds

1 pound ground pork

½ red apple, diced

2 tablespoons maple syrup

1 teaspoon garlic powder

1 teaspoon onion powder

1 teaspoon paprika

1 teaspoon fine sea salt

½ teaspoon ground sage

½ teaspoon red pepper flakes

½ teaspoon dried rosemary

¼ teaspoon black pepper

3 tablespoons butter, ghee, or coconut oil

1. In a small sauté pan over medium heat, toast the fennel seeds for no more than 5 minutes, until fragrant.

2. Place all the ingredients except the butter in a large bowl and mix until well combined.

3. Divide the sausage mixture into 8 patties and flatten them between your hands.

4. In a large cast-iron skillet over low heat, melt the butter. Add 3 or 4 patties to the pan and cook for 5 to 6 minutes per side, until golden brown and cooked through. Keeping the heat on low will help cook the insides of the patties without burning the outsides. Patience is key here.

Put this sausage on:

Breakfast Tacos (page 70)

Pulled Pork Benedict with Green Chile Hollandaise (page 74)

Individual Breakfast Pizzas (page 64)

individual
breakfast pizzas

Yield: 3 pizzas (serving 3 to 6)

Prep time: 10 minutes, plus time to precook the crusts and make the pesto

Cook time: 10 to 35 minutes per pizza

3 pizza crusts, individual breakfast pizza version (page 288)

for the pesto prosciutto pizza:

¼ cup Dairy-Free Pesto (page 280)

½ large heirloom tomato, thinly sliced

4 slices prosciutto

1 large egg

fine sea salt and black pepper

for the sausage and mushroom pizza:

2 slices bacon, diced

4 ounces chorizo

¼ cup sliced button mushrooms

1 large egg

fine sea salt and black pepper

for the sweet potato, bacon, and sausage pizza:

2 slices bacon

½ small sweet potato or yam, shredded

4 ounces breakfast sausage

½ red bell pepper, diced

1 large egg

fine sea salt and black pepper

Now let's get one thing straight: I think all pizzas should include an egg on them and not be considered breakfast. *Because a runny egg is just sauce. And everyone loves sauce.* I used to dip my pizza in ranch dressing (and sometimes still do; you'll find the recipe on page 272). Because ranch is a sauce, and therefore it is amazing. Here you have breakfast, pizza, and sauce all rolled into one meal. AHHHHHHH, IT'S SO AMAZING!

1   Make the crusts. After the crusts are cooked, reduce the oven temperature to 325°F.

2   **For the pesto prosciutto pizza:** Place the cooked crust on a baking sheet. Spread the pesto on the crust, then the sliced tomatoes and prosciutto.

3   **For the sausage and mushroom pizza:** Place the cooked crust on a baking sheet. In a small sauté pan over medium heat, cook the bacon until crispy, about 10 minutes, then remove from the pan and set aside. Add the chorizo to the pan and cook for 10 minutes, breaking it into small pieces with a wooden spoon, until almost cooked through. Add the sliced mushrooms and cook for 3 minutes, until the mushrooms are soft. Top the crust with the chorizo mixture, then the bacon.

4   **For the sweet potato, bacon, and sausage pizza:** Place the cooked crust on a baking sheet. In a small sauté pan over medium heat, cook the bacon until crispy, about 10 minutes, then remove from the pan and set aside. Add the shredded sweet potato to the pan and cook for about 6 minutes, until soft, then set aside with the bacon. Add the sausage and bell pepper and cook for about 10 minutes, until the sausage is cooked through. Top the crust with the sweet potato, then the sausage mixture, then the bacon.

5   Press the middle of each pizza in a bit to create a nest, then crack an egg into it. Season with salt and pepper, place on the upper rack of the oven, and bake for 8 to 10 minutes, until the egg is cooked to your liking.

prosciutto herb
frittata

Serves: 8

Prep time: 5 minutes

Cook time: 20 minutes

● ● ● ●

Frittatas are one of my favorite things because they sound fancy—ooh, fri-tta-ta—but they are really just whisked eggs baked without a crust. It doesn't get any easier. *I make frittatas at home on a regular basis because I hate cooking in the morning.* Most of the time, that's what I do all day long. So I would much rather reheat a slice of leftover fancy frittata and get on with my day.

8 large eggs

2 tablespoons full-fat coconut milk

1 cup chopped fresh spinach

1 tablespoon finely chopped fresh parsley

1 tablespoon finely chopped fresh chives

1 teaspoon finely chopped fresh thyme

1 teaspoon fine sea salt

¼ teaspoon black pepper

1 ounce (about 4 slices) prosciutto, torn

1. Preheat the oven to 325°F. Grease a large cast-iron skillet.

2. In a large bowl, whisk together the eggs, coconut milk, spinach, herbs, salt, and pepper. Pour the mixture into the skillet. Distribute the torn pieces of prosciutto throughout the egg mixture, pushing it down into the eggs.

3. Bake for 18 to 20 minutes, until set in the middle and no longer jiggly.

You may also like:

Breakfast Tacos
(page 70)

Pulled Pork Benedict with Green Chile Hollandaise
(page 74)

Apple Fennel Breakfast Sausage
(page 62)

breakfast tacos

Yield: 12 tacos (serving 4)

Prep time: 5 minutes, plus time to make the tortillas, sweet potatoes, and hollandaise

Cook time: 15 minutes

1 pound bacon

10 large eggs

½ teaspoon fine sea salt

¼ teaspoon black pepper

1 batch Tortillas (page 290)

1 batch Spicy Sweet Potatoes (page 186)

1 batch Hollandaise (page 276)

chopped fresh chives, for garnish

After making breakfast tacos at Lake Powell a couple years ago, I became obsessed with everything taco related. *What is it about being wrapped in a tortilla that makes food taste so much better?* I don't know, but I'm into it.

1. In a large sauté pan over medium heat, cook the bacon until crispy, about 10 minutes. Set aside on a paper towel, then remove the excess bacon fat from the pan, leaving about 2 to 3 tablespoons in the pan.

2. Reduce the heat to low. Whisk the eggs, then pour them into the pan and sprinkle with the salt and pepper. Continuously whisk the eggs with a spatula to keep them fluffy, cooking until they are cooked through but still soft, about 5 minutes.

3. Assemble the tacos: Top each tortilla with 4 or 5 spicy sweet potatoes, using a fork to smash them down, then layer on 1 or 2 slices of bacon, scrambled eggs, and hollandaise. Garnish with fresh chives.

Tasty tips:

- If you hate making tortillas or you ain't got time, check out Must B Nutty tortillas online. They are the best things out there!

- Don't be afraid to add toppings like salsa, hot sauce, chorizo, avocado, cilantro, or shredded short ribs (page 108)— whatever your heart desires! The world is your oyster, "the world" meaning your taco.

Try these different meats in your breakfast tacos:

Slow Cooker Short Rib Tostadas (page 108)

Lechón Asado (page 138)

Carne Mechada (page 122)

pulled pork benedict
with green chile hollandaise

Serves: 4

Prep time: 10 minutes

Cook time: 6 to 8 hours

1 (2-pound) boneless pork butt or shoulder

3 cloves garlic

1 cup vegetable broth

fine sea salt

2 large sweet potatoes or yams, cut into 1-inch slices (you'll need 8 thick slices)

2 to 3 tablespoons ghee, butter, or coconut oil, melted

1 batch Green Chile Hollandaise (below)

6 large eggs

black pepper

● Make the pork overnight so it's ready to go in the morning and can stay warm in your slow cooker while you finish up the rest of the recipe.

● If green chiles are in season, roast the chiles, peel them, and then chop them up small for your hollandaise. They are so much more flavorful than the canned kind.

I'm a *huge hollandaise fan.* I can't get enough of it. I'll eat it on hash, eggs, even a steak. And when I finally made hollandaise for the first time and figured out how easy it is, I was completely sold on eating it on a weekly basis. Try putting hollandaise on everything; you won't regret it.

① Slice 3 small slits in the pork and press the garlic cloves into the slits. Place the pork in a slow cooker, pour in the broth, and then sprinkle the top of the pork generously with salt. Cover and cook on low for 6 to 8 hours, until fork-tender. Once cooked through, shred the meat with 2 forks and keep warm over low heat.

② About 45 minutes before the pork is done, preheat the oven to 400°F. Set a wire rack on top of a baking sheet. Cover each sweet potato slice with melted ghee and sprinkle with salt. Place on the wire rack and bake for 30 to 35 minutes, flipping once midway through the cooking time.

③ When the sweet potatoes are halfway done, make the hollandaise.

④ Make the poached eggs: Break each egg into a small cup, transfer it to a wire mesh strainer, swirl it around to get rid of the excess whites, and then return it to the cup. Bring a stockpot of salted water to a low boil over medium heat. Slowly ease each egg into the pot, spacing them evenly. After about 15 seconds, gently start swirling them around with a spoon or spatula. Continue to move them to help the shape, but make sure not to break them. After about 3 minutes, the whites should be fully set with the yolks still tender. Use a slotted spoon to scoop out each poached egg.

⑤ Top each sweet potato slice with about 2 tablespoons of pulled pork, a poached egg, some hollandaise, and some freshly cracked black pepper.

green chile hollandaise (makes ½ cup)

1 (4-ounce) can diced mild green chiles

pinch of fine sea salt

1 batch Hollandaise (page 276)

① Place the chiles in a small saucepan over medium heat. Sprinkle with a pinch of salt and cook for 2 to 3 minutes, until warmed through. Fold the chiles into the hollandaise until well combined.

poultry

Don't be a chicken.

To me, chicken and turkey are pretty much the worst. They are boring, they don't have much flavor, and they remind me of the days when I tried to diet and would eat close to nothing, and that included bland chicken. But nobody puts poultry in a corner—not even this hateful bitch named Juli Bauer.

Chicken should have its day; turkey should shine from within! So that's what I'm doing here. I've added a ton of spices, flavors, and saucy sauces to these poultry dishes so they don't taste like diet food. Dear poultry, you're welcome.

buffalo chicken
casserole

Serves: 4

Prep time: 15 minutes

Cook time: 1 hour 50 minutes

A couple years ago, I posted a recipe called Spaghetti Pizza Pie on my blog. I don't know if it was the word *pizza* or that it includes only five ingredients, but people went cuckoo for Coco Puffs over that recipe. It became my top-searched recipe overnight, and it still is! *But the best part about this recipe is that it is incredibly versatile.* You can make all kinds of different casseroles with the same base—like the recipe you'll find on page 94.

1 medium spaghetti squash (about 2½ pounds)

4 tablespoons butter, ghee, or coconut oil, divided

2 cloves garlic, minced

1 medium carrot, diced

2 stalks celery, diced

½ medium yellow onion, minced

1 small red bell pepper, diced

1 pound ground chicken

1 teaspoon garlic powder

1 teaspoon fine sea salt

¼ teaspoon black pepper

1 cup hot sauce (I prefer Tessemae's or Frank's RedHot)

¼ cup Super Simple Mayonnaise (page 274) or store-bought mayo (I use Sir Kensington's or Primal Kitchen Foods)

3 large eggs, whisked

chopped scallions, for garnish

sliced avocado, for garnish

1. Preheat the oven to 400°F.

2. Cut the spaghetti squash in half lengthwise. Place the squash cut side down on a baking sheet and bake for 30 to 35 minutes or until the skin gives when you press your finger to it. Remove the squash from the oven and reduce the oven temperature to 350°F.

3. Grease a Dutch oven or an 8-inch square glass baking dish with 2 tablespoons of the butter.

4. Let the squash cool for 5 minutes, remove the seeds, and then use a fork to remove the threads and place them in the greased baking dish.

5. In a large sauté pan over medium heat, melt the remaining 2 tablespoons of butter. Add the garlic, carrot, celery, onion, and bell pepper and cook for about 10 minutes, until the onion is translucent. Add the ground chicken, garlic powder, salt, and pepper and cook, using a wooden spatula to break up the chicken into small pieces, until the chicken is no longer pink, about 8 minutes.

6. Remove the pan from the heat, then add the hot sauce and mayo and mix well to combine.

7. Add the chicken mixture to the baking dish and mix well with the spaghetti squash threads. Add the whisked eggs and mix everything together until you can no longer see the eggs.

8. Bake for 1 hour or until the top forms a slight crust that doesn't give when you press it in the middle. Let rest for 5 minutes before serving. Garnish with chopped scallion and avocado slices.

sticky sesame teriyaki
chicken wings

Serves: 4

Prep time: 5 minutes

Cook time: 50 minutes

I love these damn wings. There's no denying it. It's hard to pick a favorite recipe in a cookbook that you created yourself, but I'll put this one in my top five. The wings get super crispy, and the sauce is super saucy. *It's just magical.* Remember about licking your fingers, though; we went over this on page 33.

2 pounds chicken wings and/or drumsticks

1 teaspoon coarse sea salt

½ teaspoon black pepper

2 tablespoons melted coconut oil, butter, or ghee

2 cloves garlic, minced

1 teaspoon grated fresh ginger

½ cup coconut aminos

3 tablespoons honey

1 tablespoon chili sauce

1 teaspoon sesame oil

½ teaspoon fish sauce

½ cup raw cashews, roughly chopped

2 tablespoons sesame seeds

1 scallion, sliced, for garnish

1. Place an oven rack in the top position and preheat the oven to 400°F. Line a baking sheet with foil and place a wire rack on top.

2. Place the chicken wings on the wire rack and sprinkle with the salt and pepper. Bake for 50 minutes or until crispy.

3. While the wings are cooking, heat the coconut oil in a large saucepan over medium heat. Add the garlic and ginger and cook until fragrant, about 2 minutes.

4. Reduce the heat to medium-low and add the coconut aminos, honey, chili sauce, sesame oil, and fish sauce. Bring to a slow boil, reduce the heat, and let the sauce reduce, whisking a couple times to keep it from burning. Once the sauce has reduced by about one-third and coats the back of a spoon, pour it into a large mixing bowl.

5. In a small sauté pan over medium heat, toast the cashews until browned, tossing them for less than 10 minutes to keep them from burning.

6. Add the crispy wings to the bowl with the sauce and toss to coat. Place the wings on a large serving plate and pour any remaining sauce over the wings. Sprinkle with the sesame seeds, then garnish with the toasted cashews and sliced scallion.

Honey Lemon Sticky Chicken (page 98)

Pineapple Sweet-and-Sour Pork Meatball Skewers (page 134)

Let's get even stickier:

loaded ranch
chicken salad wraps

Yield: 6 wraps (serving 3)

Prep time: 10 minutes, plus time to make the ranch dressing

Ranch is one of those things that makes everything better. Thankfully we can make a Paleo ranch that is pretty damn tasty. Again, *chicken is effing boring,* no doubt about it, but here, flavorful ranch dressing coats the chicken in a real nice way. Just try it. You don't even need the lettuce wrap. That's art, in my opinion. Everyone knows that lettuce wraps are close to impossible to eat. That shit goes everywhere.

1 batch Ranch Dressing (page 272; use as little or as much as you like)

2 cups diced cooked chicken, chilled (I used rotisserie chicken)

1 red bell pepper, diced small

2 stalks celery, diced small

2 medium carrots, diced small

¼ medium red onion, minced

1 avocado, diced

2 scallions, chopped

¼ teaspoon fine sea salt

⅛ teaspoon black pepper

6 to 12 leaves iceberg or butter lettuce

1. In a large bowl, mix together all the ingredients except the lettuce.

2. Wrap about ¼ to ⅓ cup of the chicken mixture in 1 or 2 lettuce leaves, similar to how you would wrap a burrito.

3. Store any leftover wraps in a closed container in the refrigerator for up to 1 week.

Tasty tips:

- I made this recipe using everything I had left in the refrigerator. You can do the same with your own salad. Add whatever you have on hand. Try roasted poblano peppers, jalapeños, tomatoes, avocado, and cilantro along with your ranch dressing—you're going to love it!

- Don't want a wrap? That's fine—just throw the chicken mixture on top of some lettuce and you have a great salad!

coconut cashew chicken fingers
with spicy mango dipping sauce

Serves: 5

Prep time: 10 minutes

Cook time: 15 minutes

1 cup unsweetened coconut flakes

½ cup raw cashews

1½ teaspoons fine sea salt

1 teaspoon garlic powder

½ teaspoon paprika

¼ teaspoon cayenne pepper

1 large egg

1 tablespoon lime juice (about ½ lime)

1½ pounds boneless, skinless chicken breasts, cut into strips

4 tablespoons cup coconut oil, butter, or ghee, divided

1 batch Spicy Mango Dipping Sauce (below)

I have a similar recipe on my blog, and people dig it because their kids will eat it. I don't have kids, so I know nothing about their taste buds. I do know that my French bulldog, who is still a puppy, will eat these. *Dogs and kids are pretty much the same, right?* I thought so.

1. Preheat the oven to 350°F.

2. Place the coconut flakes, cashews, salt, garlic powder, paprika, and cayenne pepper in a food processor and pulse until well combined. Transfer to a shallow bowl.

3. In another shallow bowl, whisk together the egg and lime juice.

4. Dredge the chicken strips in the whisked egg mixture, then in the coconut mixture. Coat each strip on all sides, then set aside on a plate.

5. In a large sauté pan over medium heat, melt a tablespoon or two of coconut oil. When the pan is very hot, add the chicken strips without crowding the pan. Cook for about 1 minute per side, until browned. You may need to do this in 2 or 3 batches depending on how big the strips are and/or how big your pan is.

6. Place the browned chicken strips on a wire rack set on top of a baking sheet. This will help them cook on both sides without getting soggy. (If you don't have a rack, just flip them halfway through baking.) Bake for 10 to 12 minutes or until no pink remains inside the chicken.

7. While the chicken is baking, making the dipping sauce. Serve the chicken fingers with the dipping sauce.

spicy mango dipping sauce (makes 1½ cups)

2 cups peeled and diced mango (I buy frozen mango and thaw it before using it)

juice of 1 lime (about 2 tablespoons)

2 tablespoons honey

2 teaspoons apple cider vinegar

¼ teaspoon garlic powder

¼ teaspoon red pepper flakes

¼ teaspoon chili powder

1. Place all the ingredients in a blender and puree until smooth.

2. Store any leftover sauce in a closed container in the refrigerator for up to 1 week.

super simple
oven chicken fajitas

Serves: 3 to 4

Prep time: 10 minutes

Cook time: 30 to 35 minutes

People are always asking me for simple meals. The fewer dishes, the better. *You make this recipe in one pan.* Then you can eat it out of the one pan. And only have to clean one pan. What more could you ask for, really?

1 tablespoon chili powder

1 tablespoon smoked paprika

½ teaspoon garlic powder

½ teaspoon onion powder

¼ teaspoon ground cumin

¼ teaspoon cayenne pepper

2 teaspoons fine sea salt

1 pound boneless, skinless chicken breasts, cut into thin strips

1 red bell pepper, sliced

1 orange bell pepper, sliced

1 yellow bell pepper, sliced

1 medium red onion, sliced

¼ cup butter, ghee, or coconut oil, melted

1 to 2 limes, cut into wedges

sliced avocado, for garnish

chopped fresh cilantro, for garnish (optional)

1. Preheat the oven to 400°F.

2. Mix together the spices and salt in a small bowl.

3. Place the chicken and veggies in a large cast-iron skillet or 13 by 9-inch baking dish. Pour the melted butter over them, then sprinkle the spices on top. Toss to coat the chicken and veggies evenly with the spice mixture.

4. Bake for 30 to 35 minutes, until the chicken is cooked through.

5. Garnish the fajitas with fresh-squeezed lime juice, avocado slices, and chopped cilantro, if desired.

Tasty tip:
Serve these fajitas alongside Cilantro Lime or Mexican-Style Cauliflower Rice (page 200), as well as with Tortillas (page 290).

You like simple? I'll give you more simple:

Slow Cooker Jalapeño Popper Chicken Chili (page 100)

Marinated Flank Steak with Chimichurri and Pomegranates (page 116)

Cream of Mushroom Soup (page 166)

paella

Serves: 4

Prep time: 15 minutes

Cook time: 40 minutes

I know I'm gonna get some flack for this recipe. No, this paella is not made in a special gigantic paella pan with ten humans tending to it. I wish that were the case. Nope. *I make this in a cast-iron skillet with just my own two hands.* Some people say that paella has to have clams or something else that I don't know about, but sorry, sir, that is not how I'm making mine. After eating paella at a local restaurant, I knew I had to make it. And they made theirs with shrimp, chicken, and chorizo, so that's what I did. If you feel as though I am disrespecting your paella recipe that was passed down from your great-great-great-grandpop, please take it up with someone else. Like your dog or cat. They'll listen.

4 saffron threads

¼ cup white wine or chicken broth

3 tablespoons butter, ghee, or coconut oil

1 pound boneless, skinless chicken thighs

fine sea salt

½ medium yellow onion, minced

2 cloves garlic, minced

½ pound chorizo

½ pound shrimp, peeled and deveined

1 head cauliflower, riced*

1 red bell pepper, sliced

1 (14-ounce) can diced tomatoes, drained

½ cup chicken broth

½ teaspoon smoked paprika

1 lemon, cut into wedges

chopped fresh parsley, for garnish

1. Dissolve the saffron in the wine, then set aside.

2. In a large sauté pan over medium-high heat, melt the butter. When the pan is hot, pat the chicken dry and sprinkle with salt. Cook for 5 to 6 minutes per side, until no longer pink. Set aside.

3. Add the onion and garlic to the pan and sauté until the onion is translucent, about 5 minutes. Add the chorizo, break it into small pieces with a wooden spoon, and cook through, about 10 minutes. Remove and set aside with the chicken.

4. Pat the shrimp dry and sprinkle with salt. Cook for 1 minute per side, until the shrimp curl up and turn pink. Remove and set aside with the chicken and chorizo.

5. Add the riced cauliflower, wine, bell pepper, tomatoes, chicken broth, paprika, and 1 to 2 teaspoons of salt to the pan. Mix well and simmer for about 10 minutes, until the cauliflower is soft.

6. Return the chicken, chorizo, and shrimp to the pan and cook for 3 to 5 minutes, until warmed through.

7. Squeeze a bit of lemon juice over the top and garnish with fresh parsley.

* To rice cauliflower, cut it into florets, then run through a food processor using the shredding attachment, or mince the cauliflower using a cheese grater.

chicken carbonara
casserole

Serves: 4

Prep time: 15 minutes

Cook time: 1 hour 50 minutes

● ● ● ●

Bacon in a casserole. Need I say more?

1 medium spaghetti squash (about 2½ pounds)

2 tablespoons olive oil, coconut oil, or butter, for greasing the pan

¾ pound bacon, cut into lardons*

½ medium yellow onion, minced

3 cloves garlic, minced

1 (14-ounce) can artichoke hearts, chopped

1 pound cooked chicken, finely chopped (I used rotisserie chicken)

2 cups fresh spinach, chopped

½ teaspoon garlic powder

¼ teaspoon ground nutmeg

½ teaspoon fine sea salt

¼ teaspoon black pepper

4 large eggs, whisked

chopped fresh parsley, for garnish

> * *Lardons* is just a fancy word for small strips—ya know, because I'm fancy.

1. Preheat the oven to 400°F.

2. Cut the spaghetti squash in half lengthwise. Place the squash cut side down on a baking sheet and bake for 30 to 35 minutes or until the skin gives when you press your finger to it. Remove the squash from the oven and reduce the oven temperature to 350°F.

3. Grease a Dutch oven or an 8-inch square glass baking dish with olive oil.

4. Let the squash cool for 5 minutes, remove the seeds, then use a fork to remove the threads and place them in the greased baking dish.

5. In a large sauté pan over medium heat, cook the bacon until crispy, about 10 minutes. Remove with a slotted spoon and set aside on a paper towel.

6. Remove some of the bacon fat from the pan, leaving ¼ cup in the pan. Add the onion and garlic and cook for 2 to 3 minutes, until the onion is soft and translucent. Then add the artichoke hearts, chicken, spinach, garlic powder, nutmeg, salt, and pepper and mix well. Cook for 3 to 4 minutes, until well combined.

7. Add the chicken mixture and bacon to the baking dish and mix well with the spaghetti squash threads. Add the whisked eggs and mix everything together until you can no longer see the eggs.

8. Bake for 1 hour or until the top forms a slight crust that doesn't give when you press it in the middle. Let rest for 5 minutes before serving. Garnish with fresh parsley.

turkey meatballs

Serves: 4

Prep time: 10 minutes, plus time to make the cauliflower puree

Cook time: 15 to 20 minutes

for the meatballs:

1 pound ground turkey

1 large egg

1 teaspoon garlic powder

1 teaspoon fine sea salt

1 teaspoon dried oregano

1 teaspoon dried basil

½ teaspoon onion powder

½ teaspoon black pepper

½ teaspoon red pepper flakes

for the sauce:

2 tablespoons butter, ghee, or coconut oil

½ medium yellow onion, minced

3 cloves garlic, minced

1 (24-ounce) jar tomato sauce

¼ cup chopped fresh basil, plus extra for garnish

½ to 1 teaspoon fine sea salt

1 batch Cauliflower Puree (page 202)

Once when I was watching the Food Network (when I say "Once," I mean that it's on 24/7 in my house), I saw this guy who owns a meatball shop in Canada and makes all kinds of meatballs and meatball subs. *One of the meatballs he made was paired with mashed potatoes.* It looked so freaking good, minus the breadcrumbs. That is where my recipe came from. Someday, I hope to travel to Canada just to eat one of those meatballs. Preferably in the summertime.

1. Preheat the oven to 350°F. Line a baking sheet with parchment paper.

2. Place all the ingredients for the meatballs in a large bowl and mix well to combine. Use a 1½-tablespoon cookie scoop to make 16 meatballs and place them on the lined baking sheet. Bake for 15 to 20 minutes, until completely cooked through.

3. While the meatballs are baking, make the sauce: Melt the butter in a large sauté pan over medium heat. Add the onion and garlic and cook until the onion is translucent, about 5 minutes. Add the tomato sauce, basil, and ½ teaspoon salt. Taste, then add more salt, if desired. Simmer on low heat until the meatballs are done.

4. Once the meatballs are cooked through, place them in the pan with the sauce and spoon the sauce over them. Serve the meatballs and sauce over cauliflower puree, garnished with extra basil.

Don't forget your sides:

Lemon Truffle Roasted Cauliflower (page 190)

Oven-Roasted Fennel (page 196)

honey lemon
sticky chicken

Serves: 4

Prep time: 10 minutes, plus time to make the cauliflower rice

Cook time: 35 minutes

● ● ● ●

Eating with chopsticks is a skill that I have not mastered yet. Eating cauliflower rice with chopsticks is close to impossible. No, scratch that, it's completely impossible. I don't understand how people do it on a regular basis. Even with real-deal rice. It's so damn hard. If you make this recipe, I recommend consuming it with a fork—it's just easier that way. *And the easier it is, the faster you get your food.* And everyone wants that.

3 tablespoons butter, ghee, or coconut oil

¼ medium sweet onion, minced

1 clove garlic, minced

1 pound boneless, skinless chicken breasts, diced small

1 teaspoon fine sea salt

1 teaspoon garlic powder

for the sauce:

¾ cup chicken broth

¼ cup plus 1 tablespoon honey

¼ cup lemon juice

2 tablespoons coconut aminos

1 teaspoon grated fresh ginger

1 teaspoon coconut vinegar

1 teaspoon Sriracha

1 batch Cauliflower Rice (page 200)

1 tablespoon white sesame seeds, for garnish

chopped scallions, for garnish

⅛ teaspoon black pepper

1. Melt the butter in a large sauté pan over medium heat. Add the onion and garlic and cook until the onion is translucent, about 5 minutes.

2. Season the chicken with the salt and garlic powder, then add to the pan. Brown on all sides until cooked through, about 12 minutes. Remove from the pan and set aside on a plate.

3. In a medium bowl, whisk together all the sauce ingredients.

4. Reduce the heat to medium-low and place the sauté pan back over the heat. Pour in the sauce mixture and bring to a low boil. Let the sauce reduce by about one-third, about 10 to 15 minutes, until the sauce coats the back of a spoon.

5. Once the sauce has thickened, return the chicken to the pan and cook for 2 minutes to warm the chicken through.

6. Serve over cauliflower rice, garnished with sesame seeds and chopped scallions and seasoned with pepper.

Tasty tip:
Pair this chicken with Sweet & Crunchy Green Beans (page 198).

Sticky Sesame Teriyaki Chicken Wings (page 82)

Pineapple Sweet-and-Sour Pork Meatball Skewers (page 134)

If you like sticky, you may also like:

slow cooker
jalapeño popper chicken chili

Serves: 6

Prep time: 10 minutes

Cook time: 8 hours

I hate sports. I don't like watching them, I don't like playing them. But I do like going to parties that involve a ton of food with some sort of game playing in the background. That way, I can act like I fit in with all the people watching the game while I stuff my face instead. To me, a sports party (that's what it's called, right?) just isn't a party without jalapeño poppers. You know, the jalapeño peppers stuffed with cream cheese, wrapped in bacon, and baked until soft and gooey yet crunchy? Know what I'm sayin'? This is my meal version of jalapeño poppers. Which you could totally make for your sports parties. *Go sports!*

1 medium white onion, diced

3 cloves garlic, minced

1 red bell pepper, diced

2 jalapeños, minced (remove seeds for less heat)

1 large sweet potato, diced

1 pound ground chicken

1 pound ground beef

2 teaspoons smoked paprika

2 teaspoons chili powder

2 teaspoons dried oregano

2 teaspoons fine sea salt

1 teaspoon ground cumin

½ teaspoon red pepper flakes

1 (14-ounce) can diced tomatoes

1 cup chicken or beef broth

4 ounces goat cheese, crumbled (optional)

sliced jalapeño, for garnish

chopped scallions, for garnish

1 Place all the ingredients except the goat cheese and garnishes in a slow cooker. Cover and cook on low for 8 hours.

2 At the end of the cooking time, mix in the goat cheese, if using, until completely melted into the chili.

3 Serve garnished with sliced jalapeño and chopped scallions.

Tasty tip: Sliced avocado would make a great garnish, too!

Looking for a warm, hearty meal? You may also like:

Rich & Hearty Bacon Beef Stew (page 120)

Mexican Meatloaf (page 106)

beef

Got beef?

For the longest time, meaning about 21 years on this earth, I didn't really like beef. If my beef was served in the form of a steak, I liked it even less. I thought the amount of chewing involved was exhausting. And I had a quick stint of being a vegetarian who still ate fish, so I said, "OMGEWBEEF." But then a beautiful thing happened: My taste buds changed, I learned the miracle of the slow cooker, and I began buying better cuts of meat. *And BOOM, steak became my friend.* We're still not best friends like me and pork, but we get by with a pretty good relationship.

mexican meatloaf

Serves: 6

Prep time: 15 minutes

Cook time: 1 hour 15 minutes

Meatloaf was one of the first recipes I made when I started Paleo. CrossFitters seem to love it, so *I trusted the buff weirdos and went with it.* Turns out, they were right. Meatloaf is awesome. It's a way to use up ground beef in a super flavorful way. I remember cartoons always making jokes about how gross Mom's meatloaf was. I don't know what meatloaf those cartoon characters were eating, but it obviously wasn't Paleo. Dummies.

1 pound ground beef

1 pound chorizo

1 red bell pepper, diced

½ medium white onion, minced

1 (7-ounce) can diced green chiles

2 cloves garlic, minced

½ tablespoon garlic powder

½ tablespoon onion powder

½ tablespoon paprika

1 teaspoon chili powder

½ teaspoon fine sea salt

½ teaspoon black pepper

1 cup blanched almond flour

1 large egg

¼ cup roughly chopped fresh cilantro, plus extra for garnish

2 cups salsa of choice, divided

1 Preheat the oven to 350°F. Grease a 9 by 5-inch loaf pan.

2 In a large bowl, combine all the ingredients except for the salsa.

3 Press the mixture firmly into the prepared loaf pan. Pour 1 cup of the salsa on top of the meatloaf.

4 Bake for 1 hour 15 minutes, until the meat is completely cooked through in the middle.

5 Remove the meatloaf from the oven, top with the remaining 1 cup of salsa, and garnish with extra cilantro.

Tasty tip:
Sweeten up your meatloaf with a peach or mango salsa!

This meatloaf would be great with:

Cauliflower Puree (page 202)

Cilantro Lime Cauliflower Rice (page 200)

Pico de Gallo Salad (page 180)

slow cooker
short rib tostadas

Serves: 4
Prep time: 10 minutes
Cook time: 7 to 8 hours

Yet another way to eat a taco. Can you go wrong here? Ahellsnah.

2½ pounds short ribs

2 tablespoons lime juice (about 1 lime)

2 teaspoons garlic powder

1 teaspoon onion powder

1 teaspoon chili powder

½ teaspoon ground cumin

½ teaspoon cayenne pepper

2 teaspoons fine sea salt

2 cups beef broth

1 batch Tortillas, tostada version (page 290)

2 plum tomatoes, diced

1 avocado, diced

roughly torn cilantro, for garnish

lime wedges, for garnish

1. Place the short ribs in a slow cooker and squeeze the lime juice over the ribs.

2. In a small bowl, mix together the spices and salt. Sprinkle over the ribs. Pour the beef broth around the ribs.

3. Cook on low for 7 to 8 hours, until the meat is falling off the bone.

4. About 30 minutes before serving, make the tostada version of the tortillas.

5. Remove the bones from the ribs and shred the meat directly in the liquid to keep it flavorful.

6. Top each tortilla with some meat, tomatoes, avocado, and cilantro and squeeze some lime juice over the top.

You may also like:

Mexican Meatloaf
(page 106)

Street Fish Tacos
(page 148)

Carne Mechada
(page 122)

spicy stuffed
plantains

Serves: 4

Prep time: 20 minutes

Cook time: 30 minutes

● ● ● ●

You'll find a few plantain recipes in this book. I love me some plantains. They are starchy, crunchy when needed, and sweet when wanted. *They are just so versatile.* And thanks to Quiero Arepas, my favorite gluten-free Venezuelan food truck, I can have amazing plantains whenever I want.

4 brown plantains (you want them brown for sweetness but not completely soft)

3 tablespoons ghee, coconut oil, or butter, divided

2 cloves garlic, minced

½ red bell pepper, diced

¼ medium red onion, minced

1 pound ground beef

1 teaspoon fine sea salt

1 teaspoon garlic powder

½ teaspoon chili powder

¼ teaspoon red pepper flakes

pinch of black pepper

¼ cup fresh cilantro, finely chopped, plus extra for garnish

3 tablespoons tomato paste

¼ cup crumbled goat cheese (optional)

diced avocado, for garnish

1. Preheat the oven to 350°F.

2. Cut the ends off the plantains, then remove the skins. Cut a slit down the middle of each plantain and use your fingers to pull it apart slightly to create a boat, then place in an 8-inch square baking dish.

3. Brush about 1 tablespoon of the ghee onto and into the plantains. Bake for 20 minutes, until soft to the touch.

4. While the plantains are baking, melt the remaining 2 tablespoons of ghee in a large sauté pan over medium heat. Add the garlic and sauté for about 1 minute, then add the bell pepper and onion and cook for 5 minutes, until the onion is translucent.

5. Add the ground beef to the pan and cook until browned, about 10 minutes. Then add the salt, spices, cilantro, and tomato paste and mix until well combined.

6. Use a spoon to scoop some of the mixture into each plantain boat, piling it as high as you like. Place back in the oven for 10 minutes, until heated through.

7. Serve the plantain boats garnished with goat cheese (if using), diced avocado, and cilantro.

Tasty tip:
Serve these over Mexican-Style Cauliflower Rice (page 200), with Guasacaca (page 286) on the side.

Tostones (page 212)

Maduros (page 214)

Need more plantains?

truffle mushroom
burgers

Serves: 4

Prep time: 10 minutes, plus time to make the aioli

Cook time: 25 minutes

● ● ● ●

This burger was inspired by a burger I ate once in Austin, Texas, at a restaurant called Hopdoddy. We waited in line for what seemed like hours, because everyone said that we had to go there. It was probably 10 minutes, but I was starving, okay? The thing with burger joints is that if the burger sucks without a bun, you know they suck at life. It all starts with the meat. *And Hopdoddy knows their meat.* The burger was one of the best burgers I've ever eaten. And it had a truffle aioli on top. It was just so perfect. So I made my own with all my favorite toppings. Boom.

for the burgers:

½ pound ground pork

½ pound ground beef

3 tablespoons minced yellow onion

2 cloves garlic, minced

1 large egg

1½ teaspoons fine sea salt

¼ teaspoon black pepper

for the toppings:

5 tablespoons butter, ghee, or coconut oil, divided

3 large shallots, thinly sliced

1 cup mixed mushrooms (button, shiitake, etc.), thinly sliced

4 large eggs

1 batch Truffle Aioli (page 275)

4 slices prosciutto

coarse sea salt

black pepper

1 Preheat a grill to medium heat.

2 In a large bowl, mix together all the ingredients for the burgers until well combined. Form the mixture into 4 patties, then press your thumb in the middle of each burger. Cover and place in the fridge while you prepare the toppings.

3 In a medium sauté pan over medium-low heat, melt 3 tablespoons of the butter. Add the shallots and cook for about 6 to 7 minutes, moving them around to keep them from burning. Once the shallots are soft, add the mushrooms, sprinkle with salt, and cook for another 4 to 5 minutes, until the mushrooms are soft.

4 Grill the burgers for 3 to 4 minutes per side for medium-rare. Cover with foil and let rest for 2 to 3 minutes.

5 Heat a large sauté pan over low heat. Add the remaining 2 tablespoons of butter, then crack the eggs into the pan. Cook for 6 to 8 minutes, until the whites are cooked but the yolks are still runny.

6 Top each burger with 1 to 2 tablespoons of aioli, a slice of prosciutto, some of the mushroom mixture, an egg, and a bit of coarse sea salt and pepper.

You'll totally want to eat this burger with one (or two) of these:

Oven Parsnip Fries
(page 184)

steak frites
with herb roasted garlic butter

Serves: 3

Prep time: 10 minutes

Cook time: 35 minutes

● ● ● ●

I've said it before and I'll say it again: I don't really love steak. Because too much chewing is involved. Less chewing means less time spent at a meal, which means I'm that much closer to having dessert. *Okay, it's not that I don't like steak; it's just that I like dessert more.* #problems

for the herb butter:

1 head garlic

6 tablespoons butter, room temperature

1 tablespoon minced fresh parsley

1 tablespoon minced fresh tarragon

1 tablespoon minced fresh chives

½ teaspoon coarse sea salt

for the dry rub:

1 teaspoon garlic powder

1 teaspoon onion powder

1 teaspoon fine sea salt

½ teaspoon black pepper

¼ teaspoon cayenne pepper

2 rib-eye steaks (½ to ¾ pound each)

1 batch Oven Parsnip Fries (page 184), for serving (optional)

1. Preheat the oven to 400°F.

2. Peel and discard the papery outer layers of the head of garlic, leaving intact the skins of the individual cloves. Cut ¼ inch off the end of the bulb to expose the cloves inside. Wrap in foil and bake for 30 minutes, until the cloves are golden brown and soft.

3. If you are making the parsnip fries, make them while the garlic is baking.

4. Make the herb butter: In a bowl, mix together the roasted garlic (about 8 or 9 cloves), butter, herbs, and salt using a fork. Cover and place in the refrigerator while you prepare the steaks.

5. Preheat a grill to medium heat.

6. In a wide, shallow dish, mix together the dry rub ingredients. Place the steaks in the dish and pat on both sides to coat with the dry rub.

7. Grill the steaks for 3 to 4 minutes per side for medium-rare. Cover with foil and let rest for 3 minutes before serving.

8. Top each steak with 1 to 2 tablespoons of herb butter, and serve with fries, if desired.

You may also like:

Creamy Apple Sage Brined Pork Chops (page 132)

Marinated Flank Steak with Chimichurri & Pomegranates (page 116)

marinated flank steak
with chimichurri & pomegranates

Serves: 3

Prep time: 10 minutes, plus at least 3 hours to marinate and time to make the chimichurri

Cook time: 6 minutes

1 pound flank steak

for the marinade:

⅓ cup olive oil

⅓ cup coconut aminos

¼ cup lime juice (about 2 limes)

3 cloves garlic, minced

¼ cup fresh cilantro, minced

fine sea salt

¼ teaspoon red pepper flakes

1 batch Chimichurri (page 284)

½ cup pomegranate seeds, for garnish

I know, I know, this meal looks like Christmas. Or someone's national flag. But it is just flavorful meat. Remember how I said that I hated beef for a long time until I found good-quality meat? Flank steak is a great example. Flank steak is the best because it takes no time at all to cook, and it doesn't take much jaw work to eat. You're welcome.

1. Place the steak in a 13 by 9-inch glass baking dish. In a small bowl, whisk together the marinade ingredients, then pour the marinade over the steak. Cover and set in the fridge for at least 3 hours—the longer it marinates, the better.

2. Remove the steak from the refrigerator and preheat a grill to medium heat. Once the grill has come to temperature, grill the steak for 2 to 3 minutes per side for medium-rare, depending on thickness.

3. Remove from the grill and cover with foil. While the meat is resting, make the chimichurri.

4. Thinly slice the steak against the grain, then top with the chimichurri and pomegranate seeds and serve.

If you love flavor town, try these recipes too:

Carne Mechada
(page 122)

Lechón Asado
(page 138)

simple beef
stir-fry

Serves: 3
Prep time: 15 minutes
Cook time: 35 minutes

You know when something is so easy to make that you don't think it deserves to be called a recipe? That's this one. I could have called it *Easy Recipe Recipe*, but that just didn't have the same ring to it.

1 batch Cauliflower Rice (page 200)

3 tablespoons ghee, butter, or coconut oil

2 cloves garlic, minced

1 medium yellow onion, minced

1 pound ground beef

fine sea salt

⅓ cup coconut aminos

2 tablespoons honey

½ teaspoon red pepper flakes

½ teaspoon minced fresh ginger

chopped scallions, for garnish

1. Make the cauliflower rice and keep it warm on the stovetop over low heat.

2. Melt the ghee in a large sauté pan over medium heat. Add the garlic and cook for about 2 minutes, until fragrant. Add the onion and cook for about 5 minutes, until translucent.

3. Add the ground beef and a pinch of salt. Brown the beef, breaking it apart with a wooden spoon, until cooked through, about 10 minutes. Drain the excess fat, then place the pan back over medium heat. Add the coconut aminos, honey, red pepper flakes, and ginger, season with salt, and cook until the liquid has reduced by one-third, about 10 minutes.

4. Serve over the cauliflower rice, garnished with chopped scallions.

If you want simple, I'll give you more simple:

Slow Cooker
Jalapeño Popper
Chicken Chili
(page 100)

Fall-Off-the-Bone
Slow Cooker
Baby Back Ribs
(page 126)

Pesto Shrimp & Rice
Stuffed Peppers
(page 158)

rich & hearty
bacon beef stew

Serves: 4 to 5

Prep time: 20 minutes

Cook time: 2 hours 10 minutes

Stew meat is super cheap, but it's super damn chewy. So it needs to be cooked for a while. *If you're snowed in or you just want a hearty meal, this one will hit the spot.* Along with homemade cookies (like my Two-Toned Chewy Cookies on page 224), but that's just personal preference.

½ pound bacon, cut into lardons

1½ pounds beef stew meat

fine sea salt and black pepper

3 cloves garlic, minced

1 large yellow onion, chopped

4 large carrots, chopped

3 stalks celery, chopped

3 medium parsnips, peeled and chopped

1 teaspoon garlic powder

1 teaspoon dried thyme

½ teaspoon dried rosemary

1 cup red wine

1 quart (32 ounces) beef broth

1 (6-ounce) can tomato paste

2 tablespoons coconut aminos

1 bay leaf

2 cups button mushrooms, quartered

1 batch Cauliflower Puree (page 202)

1 In a large, heavy-bottomed pot over medium heat, cook the bacon until crispy, about 10 minutes. Remove with a slotted spoon and set aside.

2 Season the meat with salt and pepper and place in the pot. Cook until browned on all sides, about 10 minutes. Remove from the pot and set aside.

3 Place the garlic in the pot and cook for 2 to 3 minutes, until fragrant. Add the onion, carrots, celery, and parsnips. Sprinkle the vegetables with 1 teaspoon of salt along with the garlic powder, thyme, and rosemary and mix with a spoon.

4 Pour in the wine, beef broth, tomato paste, and coconut aminos and add the bay leaf. Return the meat to the pot and mix everything together. Reduce the heat, cover, and simmer for 1½ hours. While the stew is simmering, make the cauliflower puree.

5 Add the mushrooms to the stew and cook, uncovered, for another 10 minutes to help thicken the sauce.

6 Remove the bay leaf, then add the bacon to the pot and mix well to combine.

7 Serve the stew over the cauliflower puree.

Carne Mechada (page 122)

Lechón Asado (page 138)

Pulled Pork Benedict with Green Chile Hollandaise (page 74)

Other recipes slow-cooked to perfection:

carne mechada
(venezuelan beef)

Serves: 4

Prep time: 15 minutes, plus time to make the tostones and guasacaca

Cook time: 2 hours 45 minutes

This recipe is inspired by my favorite food truck in Denver, Quiero Arepas. It's a Venezuelan food truck that serves arepas, which are little sandwiches stuffed with all kinds of meat, avocado, plantains, beans, and cheeses. They aren't Paleo, but they are gluten-free goodness, and I enjoy them on a regular basis. *They even catered our engagement party!* I wanted to show you how amazing Venezuelan food is, even without the delicious bread. But if you are ever in Denver, you have to try Quiero Arepas. Truly amazing.

1 to 1½ pounds flank steak or strip steak, pounded thin

4 to 5 cups beef broth

1½ teaspoons fine sea salt, divided

2 tablespoons ghee, butter, or coconut oil

1 medium white onion, minced

1 green bell pepper, diced

3 cloves garlic, minced

1 (8-ounce) can tomato sauce

1 (6-ounce) can tomato paste

1 tablespoon coconut aminos

1 teaspoon dried oregano

½ teaspoon garlic powder

½ teaspoon smoked paprika

½ teaspoon ground cumin

2 bay leaves

1 batch Tostones (page 212)

1 batch Guasacaca (page 286)

1. Cut the steak into 6 to 8 pieces.

2. Place the beef broth in a Dutch oven over medium-high heat. When it begins to boil, add the steak and 1 teaspoon of the salt and cook, uncovered, for 15 minutes. Then cover and cook for about 2 hours, until the meat is fully cooked and fork-tender. As the meat cooks, check the broth level and add more broth if needed (the meat should always be covered by broth).

3. When the meat is ready, carefully remove it from the pot and place it on a plate. Reserve the broth (about 3 to 4 cups should remain). Use 2 forks to shred the meat.

4. Place the ghee in a large skillet over medium heat. Add the onion and bell pepper and sauté for 3 to 5 minutes, until the onion is translucent. Add the garlic and cook for 1 more minute, until fragrant. Stir in the shredded beef and mix well.

5. In a medium bowl, combine the tomato sauce, tomato paste, coconut aminos, oregano, remaining ½ teaspoon of salt, spices, and reserved broth; mix until everything is well incorporated. Add this mixture to the meat. Add the bay leaves, cover, and cook for 20 to 25 minutes, until most of the liquid has evaporated.

6. Remove the bay leaves and stir before serving to fully combine. Serve on top of tostones, drizzled with guasacaca.

pork & lamb

A pig and a sheep walk into a bar...

Don't ask me why pork and lamb are lumped together in the same section. Just don't. Some things you just shouldn't question, okay? Okay. Wait, both animals do have the cutest babies. Yep, that's why they are together.

Pork has made a comeback. For a while there, America lost its dignity and feared everything that included fat. Butter was put on the blacklist, steak was thrown in the trash, and bacon was made a mockery of as everyone bought only turkey bacon. Sadness was quite evident at the grocery store.

I remember in college, trying to figure out what healthy meant, and buying everything that was labeled fat-free, egg whites only, 100 calories or less. I was that undignified American who feared fat. I honestly don't think I bought bacon until I was 22 years old. For so long, I thought healthy meant no flavor, no calories, and no happiness. If it weren't for Paleo, I would still feel that way. But now I eat steak, I eat bacon, and I cook my food in butter, and I am the healthiest, leanest, and happiest I've ever been. Eyes are opening and bacon is sizzling. *High five, America.*

fall-off-the-bone
slow cooker baby back ribs

Serves: 5

Prep time: 10 minutes, plus time to make the BBQ sauce

Cook time: 7 to 8 hours

● ● ● ●

½ cup coconut sugar

3 tablespoons fine sea salt

1 tablespoon paprika

1 tablespoon garlic powder

1 tablespoon onion powder

1 teaspoon chili powder

1 teaspoon black pepper

1 rack baby back ribs (about 3 pounds)

1½ cups BBQ Sauce (page 278), divided

This past year, while I was visiting Austin, Texas, my friend Vanessa talked me into going to Franklin BBQ at 6:30am to wait until 11am to try their famous brisket, ribs, and pulled pork. What made it worse than waking up at 6am on vacation was that it was pouring rain that day. So we stumbled to Franklin BBQ with our frightening no-makeup faces, in the rain, to wait . . . and wait . . . and wait. *We played games, told inappropriate stories, and drank some champagne to celebrate our meat party.* I thought all this waiting for meat was ridiculous until I walked into the small Franklin building, was greeted by Aaron Franklin himself, and tried the amazing food. Am I telling you this because these ribs taste like Franklin's ribs that have been smoking for days? Nope; it's just a fun story. These ribs are delicious, though; they fall off the bone. Coolstorybye.

1. In a small bowl, mix together the coconut sugar, salt, and spices.

2. Place the ribs on a baking sheet, pour half of the spice mixture on top, and massage the spices into the meat. Flip the ribs over and repeat with the rest of the spice mixture. Press any spices that fall off into the ribs as best you can.

3. Place the ribs in a slow cooker, meaty side facing the wall, bones facing the inside. Pour 1 cup of the BBQ sauce over the ribs. Cover and cook on low for 7 to 8 hours, until the meat is falling off the bone.

4. Carefully remove the ribs from the slow cooker and place on a baking sheet. Turn the broiler on high and broil the ribs for 5 minutes, until the ribs are browned on top, but not burned.

5. Serve with the remaining ½ cup of BBQ sauce on the side.

Eat these ribs with:

Sweet & Crunchy Green Beans (page 198)

Cauliflower Puree (page 202)

maple bacon
pork loin

Serves: 4

Prep time: 10 minutes

Cook time: 35 to 40 minutes

Since I cooked most of my recipes for this book in Pittsburgh while working with Bill and Hayley on the photography, my fiancé wasn't able to try a lot of them. But this one he did get to try, and he absolutely loved it. He has requested it multiple times, and that's coming from a man who usually asks for steak and Brussels sprouts. *It's the greatest feeling when he loves what I cook!* Can you tell I'm newly engaged? Ugh, I'll stop being annoying now.

for the pork:

1 teaspoon garlic powder

1 teaspoon smoked paprika

1 teaspoon fine sea salt

½ teaspoon black pepper

1 (1½-pound) pork tenderloin

4 slices bacon

for the sauce:

¼ cup maple syrup

3 tablespoons water

2 tablespoons molasses

⅛ teaspoon chili powder

⅛ teaspoon fine sea salt

① Preheat the oven to 400°F. Line a baking sheet with parchment paper.

② In a small bowl, mix together the garlic powder, smoked paprika, salt, and pepper. Pat the pork tenderloin dry, then coat the pork with the spice mixture, pressing it into the meat.

③ In a large sauté pan over medium heat, cook the bacon until crispy, about 10 minutes. Remove from the pan and set aside on a paper towel.

④ In the same pan over medium-high heat, sear the pork on all sides in the bacon fat, about 2 minutes per side (8 minutes total).

⑤ Place the seared pork on the lined baking sheet and put it in the oven to roast for 12 to 15 minutes, until it reaches an internal temperature of 145°F.

⑥ Cover the pork with foil and let rest for 3 to 5 minutes. While the pork is resting, make the sauce: Place the sauté pan over low heat, add the sauce ingredients, and scrape the bottom of the pan. Mix together and simmer for 3 to 5 minutes, until thickened. Chop the cooked bacon into small pieces and add to the thickened sauce in the pan.

⑦ Pour the sauce over the pork, slice, and serve.

You'll love your pork loin with:

Oven Roasted Fennel
(page 196)

Spicy Sweet Potatoes
(page 186)

moo shu
pork

Serves: 3 to 4

Prep time: 40 minutes

Cook time: 20 minutes

● ● ● ●

1 batch Tortillas, moo shu pork version (page 290)

1 batch Hoisin Sauce (page 282)

for the moo shu pork:

2 tablespoons ghee, butter, or coconut oil

3 large eggs, whisked

1 teaspoon toasted sesame oil

1 (1-pound) pork tenderloin, thinly sliced

1 cup shiitake mushrooms, roughly chopped

½ cup bamboo shoots, thinly sliced

2 cups thinly sliced napa cabbage (white or purple cabbage will do also)

3 tablespoons coconut aminos

⅛ teaspoon fine sea salt

pinch of black pepper

2 scallions, chopped, plus extra for garnish

Tasty tip:
Serve with
Quick Fried Rice
(page 200).

This recipe truly has some nostalgia to it. When I was growing up, my parents and I would go to a Chinese restaurant almost every Friday. It was our little tradition. We would always get the moo shu pork, and it was my favorite thing. Now, you have to understand what a big deal this was, since I ate only packaged foods and desserts at that point. My parents were probably so happy to get some sort of protein in me, even if it included some MSG. I'm guessing that I loved moo shu pork so much because it involved little pancakes. Which are pretty much tortillas. And as you may know, I *love* tortillas. Man, I love this recipe. Seriously, *LOVE.*

1. Make the moo shu pork version of the tortillas.

2. Make the hoisin sauce. While the sauce is reducing, melt the ghee in a large sauté pan over medium heat. Add the eggs and cook until soft, about 3 minutes. Remove from the pan and set aside.

3. In the same pan, combine the sesame oil and sliced pork. Cook until white begins to appear on all sides of the pork, about 6 minutes, then add the mushrooms, bamboo shoots, cabbage, and coconut aminos. Mix well and cook until the mushrooms begin to soften, about 10 minutes, then mix in the scrambled eggs, salt, pepper, and scallions. Cook for 2 minutes, until the eggs are heated through.

4. Add half of the thickened hoisin sauce to the pan and mix well to coat.

5. Wrap ¼ to ½ cup of the mixture in a tortilla, top with hoisin sauce, and garnish with chopped scallions.

Try these other Asian-inspired meals:

Sticky Sesame Teriyaki Chicken Wings (page 82)

Honey Lemon Sticky Chicken (page 98)

Pineapple Sweet-and-Sour Pork Meatball Skewers (page 134)

creamy apple sage
brined pork chops

Serves: 4

Prep time: 10 minutes, plus 2 hours to brine

Cook time: 25 minutes

I will never go back to eating pork chops that weren't brined. *They should always be brined.* These are so damn good.

for the brine:

2 cups water

2 cups apple juice

2 tablespoons fine sea salt

1 tablespoon dried thyme

½ teaspoon black pepper

4 thin-cut, bone-in pork chops

1 teaspoon garlic powder

½ teaspoon fine sea salt

2 cloves garlic, minced

1 tablespoon butter

1 tablespoon olive oil

¼ medium sweet onion, minced

1 (5.5-ounce) can full-fat coconut milk

2 apples, cored and sliced

1 tablespoon minced fresh sage

1 tablespoon honey

1 teaspoon apple cider vinegar

fine sea salt and black pepper

1. In a 13 by 9-inch baking dish, whisk together all the ingredients for the brine. Submerge the pork chops in the liquid, cover with foil, and refrigerate for 2 hours (no more than 2 hours).

2. Pat the pork chops slightly dry, then sprinkle evenly with the garlic powder and salt.

3. In a large sauté pan over medium heat, cook the garlic in the butter and olive oil until fragrant, about 3 minutes. Add the pork chops and cook for about 3 to 4 minutes per side, depending on thickness, until browned. Set aside on a plate and cover with foil.

4. Keeping the pan over medium heat, add the onion and sauté until translucent, about 5 minutes.

5. Pour in the coconut milk and mix well. Then add the apples, sage, honey, and vinegar and season with salt and pepper. Whisk together, scraping the bottom of the pan. Bring to a low boil, then reduce the heat and let the apples soften and the liquid reduce. Once the liquid has reduced by one-third (about 8 minutes), add the pork chops, pressing them underneath the apples. Cook for 2 to 3 minutes to allow some of the mixture to seep into the meat. Serve immediately.

Cauliflower Puree (page 202)

Rosemary Roasted Beets (page 192)

Pair your pork chops with:

pineapple sweet-and-sour
pork meatball skewers

Serves: 3 to 5

Prep time: 10 minutes

Cook time: 20 to 25 minutes

for the meatballs:

1 pound ground pork

¼ medium yellow onion, minced

½ teaspoon fine sea salt

½ teaspoon garlic powder

¼ teaspoon powdered ginger

¼ teaspoon black pepper

¼ teaspoon red pepper flakes

for the sweet-and-sour sauce:

½ cup pineapple juice

¼ cup coconut vinegar

¼ cup ketchup

2 tablespoons coconut aminos

½ teaspoon powdered ginger

½ teaspoon red pepper flakes

½ teaspoon garlic powder

for the skewers:

1 red bell pepper, cut into chunks

2 cups pineapple chunks

There is something so exciting about a meatball.
It's way more fun than ground meat cooked in a pan. What's even more fun is meatballs put on skewers, sauced up, AND paired with some grilled fruit. Try grilling all different kinds of fruit with your meatballs, like cantaloupe, honeydew, or even watermelon!

1. Preheat the oven to 350°F. Line a baking sheet with parchment paper.

2. Place all the ingredients for the meatballs in a bowl and mix until well combined. Use a 1½-tablespoon cookie scoop to make 12 to 15 meatballs, then shape them with your hands. Place the meatballs on the lined baking sheet, spaced about ½ inch apart, and bake for 15 minutes, until cooked through.

3. While the meatballs are cooking, preheat a grill to medium heat. Brush the grill grates with coconut oil to help prevent sticking.

4. In a medium saucepan over medium heat, whisk together the ingredients for the sweet-and-sour sauce. Bring to a low boil, then simmer for 3 to 5 minutes, until slightly thickened.

5. When the meatballs are done and have cooled enough to handle, assemble the skewers*, adding a meatball, then a chunk of pineapple, a chunk of bell pepper, another meatball, and so on. This should make about 5 skewers, depending on the length of your skewers.

6. Brush the sauce on top of each skewer, then place the skewers sauce side down on the grill. Cook on all sides for about 1 minute per side, layering a bit of sauce on each side before turning.

7. Serve skewers with the remaining sauce on the side for dipping, if you like.

* If you're using wooden skewers, soak them in water for about 30 minutes beforehand so they don't catch fire while on the grill.

the perfect
pizza

Serves: 4

Prep time: 20 minutes, plus time to make the pesto

Cook time: 15 minutes

1 Pizza Crust (page 288)

1 batch Pizza Sauce (below)

2 tablespoons Dairy-Free Pesto (page 280)

for the toppings:

½ green bell pepper, sliced

½ orange bell pepper, sliced

2 to 4 ounces prosciutto, torn

4 to 6 ounces mozzarella (optional; I used the small balls of mozzarella)

This is another recipe that my fiancé got to try a couple times and continuously requests. We even have a gluten-free pizza place down the street from us that makes AMAZING pizzas, and he still prefers this one. I'm cool with it since he does the dishes. *Life is all about balance,* with pizza, cooking, and dishes.

1. Make the crust. While the crust is baking, make the pizza sauce. Mix the pesto into the pizza sauce until combined.

2. When the crust is done, turn up the oven temperature to 425°F.

3. Layer the crust with the sauce, bell pepper slices, prosciutto, and mozzarella, if using. Bake for 12 to 15 minutes, until the cheese melts and browns a bit or the veggies have softened and cooked through.

Variations:

BBQ Pizza: Use leftover shredded short ribs from page 108, top with extra BBQ sauce, and add some sliced red onions.

Buffalo Chicken Pizza: Use cooked, shredded chicken, hot sauce, chopped scallions, and a little goat cheese (optional).

My Favorite Flavor Pizza: Use caramelized onions (page 279) and butternut squash, bacon, and a little goat cheese (optional).

pizza sauce (makes 1 cup)

2 tablespoons olive oil

1 small white onion, minced

2 cloves garlic, minced

2 tablespoons minced sun-dried tomatoes in oil

1 (6-ounce) can tomato paste

1 cup water

3 tablespoons minced fresh basil

2 teaspoons dried oregano

½ teaspoon fine sea salt

¼ teaspoon black pepper

1. Heat the olive oil in a medium sauté pan over medium heat. Add the onion and garlic and cook until the onion is soft and translucent, about 5 minutes.

2. Add the sun-dried tomatoes and sauté for about 2 minutes, until fragrant.

3. Add the remaining ingredients and bring to a low boil. Reduce the heat to low and allow to thicken for about 10 minutes.

4. Store in a sealed container in the refrigerator for up to 1 week.

lechón asado
(slow cooker cuban pork)

Serves: 4

Prep time: 20 minutes, plus 8 hours to marinate

Cook time: 6 to 8 hours

● ● ● ●

I never knew that I loved Cuban food until I went to a restaurant called Cuba Cuba in Denver. The restaurant has these giant fans and light colors that make you feel like you're on vacation. Plus, the food is amazing. And the mojitos, but that's beside the point. They have plantain everything: chips, tostones, maduros. And then you end the evening with one of their sweet cortaditos that gives you a little caffeine high. You will smell like garlic for days after eating there, but it's absolutely worth it. *With this dish, I hope to take you on a Cuban vacation.*

for the mojo sauce:

1 head garlic (about 8 cloves)

½ cup olive oil

⅓ cup orange juice

¼ cup lime juice (about 2 limes)

½ teaspoon dried oregano

½ teaspoon ground cumin

pinch of fine sea salt and black pepper

1 (3-pound) bone-in pork butt or shoulder

¼ cup lime juice (about 2 limes)

1 teaspoon fine sea salt

for serving:

1 batch Pico de Gallo Salad (page 180)

1 batch Maduros (page 214)

1 lime, cut into wedges

1 Place the mojo sauce ingredients in a blender and process until smooth.

2 Place the pork in a large resealable plastic bag or bowl. Pour the lime juice over the pork, sprinkle with the salt, and then pour the mojo sauce over the top. Place the pork in the fridge to marinate overnight.

3 Place the pork in a slow cooker, pour the marinade on top, cover, and cook on low for 6 to 8 hours, until the meat is falling off the bone. Use 2 forks to shred the meat.

4 Make the salad, then the maduros.

5 Serve the pork, salad, and maduros together, pouring some of the leftover sauce from the slow cooker on top of everything. Squeeze fresh lime juice over the pork before eating.

Tasty tips:

● If you feel like going crazy, pair this dish with Cauliflower Rice (page 200) as well.

● For an even tastier experience, place the shredded meat in a hot, greased pan and sear it until it gets a little crust on the outside. This extra step makes the pork that much tastier!

pork & artichoke stuffed
portabella mushrooms

Serves: 3

Prep time: 10 minutes

Cook time: 15 minutes

● ● ● ●

Stuffing things into portabella mushroom caps was one of the first ways I removed bread from my diet. It made me feel like I was still having bread while making such a big change in my life. *It was my safety blanket bread.* Try stuffing all kinds of things in mushrooms caps, like burgers or chicken, or even make a little pizza with it. You'll love how deliciously easy it is.

1 pound ground pork

½ medium yellow onion, minced

2 cloves garlic, minced

1 teaspoon fine sea salt

½ cup artichoke hearts, chopped

1 (6-ounce) can tomato paste

½ teaspoon red pepper flakes

½ teaspoon garlic powder

2 cups fresh spinach, chopped

6 portabella mushroom caps, ribs and stems scraped out with a spoon

2 tablespoons blanched almond flour

1 tablespoon olive oil

1. Preheat the oven to 425°F. Line a baking sheet with parchment paper.

2. In a medium sauté pan over medium heat, combine the ground pork, onion, minced garlic, and salt. Cook, breaking the pork into pieces with a wooden spoon, until no pink remains, about 10 minutes.

3. Add the artichoke hearts, tomato paste, red pepper flakes, and garlic powder and mix well to combine.

4. Add the spinach, cover, and cook for about 1 minute, until the spinach has wilted, then mix to combine.

5. Scoop the mixture into the mushroom caps, dust with the almond flour, and then drizzle a bit of olive oil over each stuffed mushroom.

6. Bake the stuffed mushrooms on a wire rack set on top of the lined baking sheet for 15 minutes, until the mushrooms are soft.

Don't forget your sides!

Cauliflower Puree
(page 202)

Lemon Truffle
Roasted Cauliflower
(page 190)

lamb curry

Serves: 3

Prep time: 5 minutes, plus time to make the cauliflower rice

Cook time: 15 minutes

Curry is one of my favorite flavors because there really is no other flavor like it. I thought curry by itself was the best until Hayley told me to add in some lemon grass, and *Pow-Shazam-Boom-Clap*, mouth flavor party.

1 medium yellow onion, chopped

3 cloves garlic, minced

3 tablespoons butter, ghee, or coconut oil

1 red bell pepper, chopped

1 pound ground lamb

1 tablespoon plus 1 teaspoon yellow curry powder

½ teaspoon ground cinnamon

½ teaspoon garam masala

½ teaspoon powdered ginger

¼ teaspoon ground coriander

¼ teaspoon ground cumin

1 (14-ounce) can full-fat coconut milk

1 stalk lemon grass

1 batch Cauliflower Rice (page 200)

lime wedges, for garnish

chopped fresh cilantro, for garnish

1. In a large sauté pan over medium heat, sauté the onion and garlic in the butter until the onion is translucent, about 5 minutes.

2. Add the bell pepper and ground lamb. Cook, breaking the lamb into small pieces with a wooden spoon, until no pink remains, about 10 minutes.

3. Add the spices and coconut milk and mix well to combine. Add the lemon grass and simmer for about 5 minutes, until the lemon grass is fragrant. Remove the lemon grass before serving.

4. Serve the curry over cauliflower rice, garnished with lime wedges and chopped cilantro.

Simple Beef Stir-Fry (page 118)

Slow Cooker Jalapeño Popper Chicken Chili (page 100)

Turkey Meatballs (page 96)

You may also like:

pistachio rosemary
lamb chops

Serves: 4

Prep time: 5 minutes, plus time to make the cauliflower puree

Cook time: 10 minutes

1 cup shelled raw pistachios

1 tablespoon roughly chopped fresh rosemary

1 teaspoon garlic powder

12 lamb chops, about ¾ inch thick

fine sea salt and black pepper

3 to 4 tablespoons melted ghee, butter, or coconut oil

1 batch Cauliflower Puree (page 202)

Tasty tip:
If you want to make these chops even fancier, you could make a balsamic reduction to go on top. Ooooh, you so fancy.

For some reason, lamb chops used to intimidate me. They seem like such a refined food. And, well, I'm not exactly refined, if you haven't noticed. Even though I saw them in the grocery store, *I always glanced over them with fear.* But when Bill and Hayley grilled some in just minutes, and they were incredibly tender and flavorful, I let go of my fear and opened my arms to lamb.

1. Preheat the oven to 425°F. Line a baking sheet with parchment paper.

2. In a food processor, pulse the pistachios, rosemary, and garlic powder until finely chopped. Spread out the mixture in a shallow dish.

3. Season each lamb chop with a pinch of salt and pepper. Brush both sides of the chops with the melted ghee, press each chop firmly into the pistachio mixture to coat both sides, and then place on the lined baking sheet.

4. Roast in the oven for 5 minutes, flip, and continue to roast for an additional 5 minutes for medium-rare or 6 to 7 minutes for medium, depending on thickness. Remove from the oven, loosely cover with foil, and let rest for 3 to 5 minutes.

5. Serve the chops over cauliflower puree.

Don't forget your sides:

Rosemary Roasted Beets (page 192)

Lemon Truffle Roasted Cauliflower (page 190)

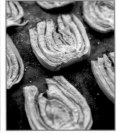

Oven-Roasted Fennel (page 196)

fish & seafood

"Just keep swimming. Just keep swimming."

The real question here is . . . when the hell is the second installment of *Finding Nemo* going to come out? Dory is my favorite Ellen of all time. Right after human Ellen.

I don't really have much to say about seafood except that I live in a landlocked state. Fish and seafood have to swim a long way to make it to my beautiful state of Colorado. Because of that, fish and seafood can be a bit creepy sometimes. But I still eat it. *Gotta do whatcha gotta do.*

street fish
tacos

Serves: 4

Prep time: 15 minutes, plus time to make the tortillas

Cook time: 10 minutes

I live near a taco place called Pinche Tacos. You should laugh if you know what *pinche* means in Spanish. Anyhoo, they make these little tacos that are *SO* flavorful. *They are some of the best tacos I've ever had.* I'll wait an hour for a table in their super loud, super tiny restaurant just to eat four tacos and be out of there in ten minutes. They're that good. I can't say mine are as good as theirs yet, but I'm working on it, okay? But Bill and Hayley absolutely loved them, so that says something!

for the avocado cream:

1 avocado

¼ cup fresh cilantro, chopped

juice of 1 lime (about 2 tablespoons)

¼ jalapeño, minced (remove seeds for less heat)

pinch of fine sea salt

for the fish:

1 tablespoon cayenne pepper

1 tablespoon paprika

2 teaspoons chili powder

½ teaspoon garlic powder

½ teaspoon fine sea salt

4 tilapia fillets (1 to 1½ pounds total)

juice of 1 lime (about 2 tablespoons)

for the slaw:

¼ medium red onion, thinly sliced

¼ head red cabbage, thinly sliced

1 scallion, chopped

¼ cup fresh cilantro, chopped

juice of 1 lime (about 2 tablespoons)

pinch of fine sea salt

for serving:

12 Tortillas (page 290)

lime wedges

roughly chopped cilantro

1. Preheat the oven to 400°F. Line a baking sheet with parchment paper.

2. Place the ingredients for the avocado cream in a food processor and puree until smooth. Scoop the mixture into a bowl, cover, and put in the refrigerator to cool.

3. In a small bowl, combine the spices and salt for the fish. Mix well.

4. Place the tilapia fillets on the lined baking sheet, pour the lime juice on top, and then sprinkle half of the spice mixture over the fish. Press the spices into the fish, then flip and repeat with the rest of the spice mixture. Bake for 10 minutes, until the fish is flaky.

5. While the fish is cooking, make the slaw: Combine all the slaw ingredients in a bowl and mix to combine the flavors.

6. When the fish is done, tear it apart slightly with a fork. Then stack the tacos: tortilla, fish, extra lime juice, slaw, avocado cream, and cilantro.

Tasty tip:
Try these tacos with Carne Mechada (page 122), Lechón Asado (page 138), or the meat from Slow Cooker Short Rib Tostadas (page 108).

hoisin salmon

Serves: 4

Prep time: 15 minutes, plus time to make the cauliflower rice

Cook time: 20 minutes

● ● ● ●

I made up this recipe completely on a whim. I had made my Moo Shu Pork (page 130) and had some extra hoisin sauce to use up. When you're making five recipes per day, the last thing you want is more food to go to waste. So I spread the sauce on some salmon and was incredibly surprised at how much I loved it. *Because it was so damn easy!* This has become my favorite way to cook salmon. Remember, the more sauce, the better. Pure science right there.

1 batch Hoisin Sauce (page 282)

4 salmon fillets (1 to 1½ pounds total)

½ teaspoon fine sea salt

1 heaping tablespoon sesame seeds

1 batch Cauliflower Rice (page 200)

chopped scallions, for garnish (optional)

1 Make the hoisin sauce.

2 Preheat the oven to 400°F. Line a baking sheet with parchment paper.

3 Place the salmon fillets on the lined baking sheet and sprinkle each fillet with salt. Use a basting brush to brush each fillet generously with the hoisin sauce. Sprinkle the sesame seeds on top of the salmon.

4 Bake for 10 minutes, until the fish is flaky and a bit translucent in the middle. Serve over cauliflower rice and garnish with scallions, if desired.

Tasty tip:
For even more flavor, serve this dish with Quick Fried Rice (page 200) instead of plain cauliflower rice.

You may also like:

Moo Shu Pork (page 130)

Pineapple Sweet-and-Sour Pork Meatball Skewers (page 134)

Sweet & Crunchy Green Beans (page 198)

mahi mahi
with mango-tomato salsa

Serves: 2

Prep time: 10 minutes, plus time to make the cauliflower rice

Cook time: 15 minutes

3 tablespoons butter, ghee, or coconut oil

2 mahi mahi fillets (¾ to 1 pound total)

½ teaspoon fine sea salt

for the salsa:

1 cup peeled and diced mango

¼ medium red onion, minced

⅓ cup halved cherry tomatoes

½ jalapeño, seeded and minced

2 tablespoons minced fresh cilantro

1 clove garlic, minced

juice of 1 lime (about 2 tablespoons)

salt to taste

cayenne pepper to taste

1 batch Cilantro Lime Cauliflower Rice (page 200)

handful of fresh spinach

Mahi mahi is probably my favorite fish to eat. *It's easy to cook, done in minutes, and tasty with almost anything.* I luuuuuuuurv eating it with mango salsa because it's such a pop of flavor. But you could also make this salsa with pineapple, strawberries, or even peaches. The mahi mahi will taste great with any of them!

1 Melt the butter in a large sauté pan over medium-high heat. Once the pan is very hot, pat the mahi mahi fillets dry and season on both sides with the salt, then place in the pan and cook for 5 to 7 minutes per side, until flaky. Do not crowd the pan, or the fish will steam instead of getting a nice crust.

2 While the fish is cooking, make the salsa: In a medium bowl, combine the salsa ingredients and mix well.

3 Serve the mahi mahi over cauliflower rice and spinach and top with the mango-tomato salsa.

You may also like:

Pico de Gallo Salad (page 180)

Street Fish Tacos (page 148)

Pulled Pork Salad with Tomatillo Ranch Dressing (page 176)

poblano cream
shrimp taquitos

Serves: 4

Prep time: 15 minutes, plus time to make the tortillas

Cook time: 35 to 40 minutes

Did you ever have one of those taquitos while picking up some gum at the 7/11? *(Did I say gum? I meant Snickers)* I never actually tried one, but as a kid I watched them twirl around on the little hot dog roller thingamajig. They never looked very appetizing to me, so I had to create my own. These taquitos are much better than those convenience store ones, I promise you.

for the poblano cream sauce:

1 poblano chile, roasted

2 avocados

½ jalapeño, seeded and minced

¼ cup fresh cilantro leaves, plus extra for garnish

3 tablespoons full-fat coconut milk

3 tablespoons vegetable broth

¼ teaspoon ground cumin

fine sea salt and black pepper

juice of ½ lemon (about 1½ tablespoons)

juice of ½ lime (about 1 tablespoon)

for the shrimp:

2 tablespoons butter, ghee, or coconut oil, plus extra for brushing

½ medium yellow onion, minced

2 cloves garlic, minced

½ jalapeño, seeded and minced

½ pound shrimp, deveined, peeled, and diced

½ teaspoon fine sea salt

juice of ½ lime (about 1 tablespoon)

1 batch Tortillas (page 290)

hot sauce, for serving (I prefer Tessemae's or Frank's RedHot)

1. Preheat the oven to 425°F. Line a baking sheet with parchment paper.

2. Turn the gas stovetop on and place the poblano chile over the flame, turning it every so often once the skin begins to blacken. Char on all sides until the skin is completely black and the poblano is soft, about 10 to 15 minutes. (If you don't have a gas stove, see the tip below.) Let cool, then rinse under cold water to remove the blackened skin and seeds. Place the roasted poblano in a food processor along with the other sauce ingredients and puree until smooth. Set aside.

3. Place the butter in a large sauté pan over medium heat. Add the onion, garlic, and jalapeño and cook until the onion is translucent, about 5 minutes. Add the shrimp, salt, and lime juice, mix well, and cook until the shrimp are pink, about 2 minutes per side. Remove from the heat, add half of the poblano cream sauce, and mix well to combine.

4. Assemble the taquitos: Place a tortilla on the lined baking sheet, add 3 to 4 tablespoons of the shrimp mixture, and roll, tucking the edges underneath to keep the taquito from opening up. Repeat with the remaining tortillas and shrimp filling. Brush each taquito with a bit of butter and bake for 15 to 18 minutes, until the outsides are crisp. Garnish with cilantro and serve with hot sauce and the remaining poblano cream sauce.

Tasty tips:

- If you don't have a gas stove, turn the broiler on and place the poblano on a foil-lined baking sheet. Broil for 10 to 15 minutes, using tongs to turn the pepper every 3 to 4 minutes.

- Be careful when picking these bad boys up; they don't hold together as well as deep-fried taquitos do.

pesto shrimp & rice
stuffed peppers

Serves: 3 to 4

Prep time: 10 minutes, plus time to make the cauliflower rice and pesto

Cook time: 15 minutes

● ● ● ●

This meal is so crazy easy. Just make it; don't think twice about it.

2 tablespoons butter, ghee, or coconut oil

½ medium yellow onion, minced

3 cloves garlic, minced

½ pound shrimp, deveined, peeled, and diced

1 batch Cauliflower Rice (page 200)

⅓ cup Dairy-Free Pesto (page 280)

½ teaspoon fine sea salt

½ teaspoon black pepper

3 red bell peppers, cut in half lengthwise, ribs and seeds removed

1 Preheat the oven to 400°F.

2 Melt the butter in a large sauté pan over medium heat. Add the onion and garlic and sauté for 3 to 4 minutes, until the onion is translucent.

3 Add the shrimp and cook until they turn pink, about 2 to 3 minutes. Add the cauliflower rice, pesto, salt, and pepper and mix well to combine.

4 Scoop the mixture into the 6 bell pepper halves. Place on a baking sheet and bake for 10 minutes, until the peppers are soft to the touch.

More quick recipes:

White Wine Butter Scallops (page 160)

Pistachio Rosemary Lamb Chops (page 144)

Simple Beef Stir-Fry (page 118)

white wine
butter scallops

Serves: 2 to 3

Prep time: 10 minutes

Cook time: 15 minutes

Personally, I love scallops just seared with a little salt and pepper. But when they're in a cookbook, *they need a bit more jazz.* And in my cookbook, that jazz comes in the form of white wine. I don't like to drink it, but I sure do like to cook with it.

1½ teaspoons butter or ghee

8 large sea scallops

¼ teaspoon fine sea salt

½ cup white wine

2 tablespoons vegetable broth

2 cloves garlic, minced

2 tablespoons minced sweet onion

3 tablespoons cold butter or ghee

2 tablespoons cup fresh parsley, roughly chopped

1 tablespoon lemon juice

1 tablespoon chopped scallion

black pepper

1 In a medium sauté pan over medium heat, melt 1½ teaspoons of butter. Season the scallops on both sides with the salt, then place in the hot pan. Sear for 3 to 4 minutes per side or until browned. Be sure not to crowd the pan; to help the scallops sear rather than steam, you may want to work in 2 batches. Transfer the seared scallops to a plate and cover with foil to keep warm.

2 With the pan still over medium heat, add the wine, broth, garlic, and onion. Bring to a boil and let the sauce reduce for 2 to 3 minutes.

3 Add the cold butter a tablespoon at a time, whisking to dissolve it completely before adding the next tablespoon.

4 Once the butter is fully incorporated, add the parsley, lemon juice, scallion, and a bit of salt and pepper. Mix well.

5 Return the scallops to the sauce and spoon the sauce over the tops of the scallops before serving.

Don't forget your sides!

Cauliflower Puree (page 202)

Cream of Mushroom Soup (page 166)

Rosemary Roasted Beets (page 192)

soups,
salads,
& sides

Sip, chomp, snack.

Personally, I'm quite content with having a bit of meat and calling it good when it comes to a meal. Sometimes cooking vegetables seems like way too much work. But I hear they're pretty good for you, so I still end up making them on the reg (that means regular; I'm so hip). In this chapter, I share my *favorite and easiest side dishes that will make your life simpler.* And more hip. Because everyone wants that.

creamy asparagus
soup

Serves: 4
Prep time: 20 minutes
Cook time: 40 minutes

● ● ● ●

This one time, I saw *a poached egg on soup* and my life changed forever. That is all.

2 tablespoons ghee, butter, or coconut oil

3 cloves garlic, minced

½ medium yellow onion, minced

2 leeks, white parts chopped small (discard the green ends)

2 bundles asparagus, ends removed, roughly chopped

1 quart (32 ounces) chicken broth

1 tablespoon fine sea salt

4 slices bacon

1 fennel bulb, thinly sliced

4 large eggs

1. In a large pot over medium heat, combine the ghee, garlic, onion, and leeks. Cook for 5 minutes, until the onion is translucent.

2. Add the asparagus, chicken broth, and salt. Bring to a low boil and cook for 15 minutes, until the asparagus is fork-tender.

3. While the asparagus is cooking, cook the bacon in a medium sauté pan over medium heat until crispy, about 10 minutes. Remove from the pan and set aside to cool slightly, then chop into small pieces. In the same pan over low heat, sauté the fennel with a pinch of salt until soft and caramelized, about 10 minutes.

4. When the asparagus is tender, reduce the heat to low and use an immersion blender to puree the soup until smooth. Keep warm over low heat.

5. Poach the eggs: Break each egg into a small cup, then transfer it to a wire mesh strainer, swirl it around to get rid of the excess whites, and return it to the original cup. Bring a stockpot of salted water to a low boil over medium heat. Slowly ease each egg into the water, spacing them evenly. After about 15 seconds, gently start swirling them around with a spoon or spatula. Continue to move them to help the shape, but make sure not to break them. After about 3 minutes, the whites should be fully set with the yolks still tender.

6. Use a slotted spoon to scoop out each poached egg. Top each bowl of soup with a poached egg and garnish with the chopped bacon and caramelized fennel.

cream of mushroom
soup

Serves: 4 to 5

Prep time: 5 minutes

Cook time: 30 minutes

When I think of soups, I want creamy soups. I don't care for simple broth-based soups like chicken noodle soup; I want density. *I want to feel like I've had a hearty meal.* Like it's sticking to my ribs. Back in college, I would go to a soup restaurant almost every day trying every creamy soup they had. This soup reminds me of those cold and windy days in college, when I spent all my money on booze and soup. Makes total sense.

3 tablespoons ghee, butter, or coconut oil

2 cloves garlic, minced

1 medium yellow onion, chopped

fine sea salt

2 cups button mushrooms, stems removed, sliced

2 cups shiitake mushrooms, stems removed, sliced

1 tablespoon fresh thyme, minced

2 cups vegetable or chicken broth

1 tablespoon tapioca flour/starch or arrowroot flour

1 cup heavy cream, full-fat coconut milk, or unsweetened almond milk*

1 bay leaf

freshly cracked black pepper

1. In a large pot over medium heat, combine the ghee and garlic. When the garlic is fragrant, about 2 minutes, add the onion along with a pinch of salt. Sauté for 5 minutes or until the onion is translucent.

2. Add the mushrooms, thyme, and another pinch of salt. Mix and cook for 5 to 7 minutes, until the mushrooms have cooked down by half. Meanwhile, in a bowl, whisk together the broth and tapioca flour, then add the broth mixture, cream, bay leaf, and another pinch of salt to the pot. Cook for 15 minutes, stirring once or twice.

3. Remove the bay leaf and serve the soup garnished with freshly cracked black pepper.

* I prefer heavy cream for this recipe because my body can handle it. If you want to make it dairy-free, canned coconut milk is best. Coconut milk can taste a little sweet, though, so be sure to check if the soup needs more salt to combat the sweetness.

You may also like:

Creamy Asparagus Soup (page 164)

White Wine Butter Scallops (page 160)

Pistachio Rosemary Lamb Chops (page 144)

thai butternut squash
soup

Serves: 3

Prep time: 35 minutes

Cook time: 10 minutes

● ● ● ●

Butternut squash, acorn squash, and sweet potato are three of my favorite starches to serve in soup form. Because all three are so sweet, pairing them with salt from meat and veggies does wonders. *Wonders, I tell you!*

1 large butternut squash

2 tablespoons ghee, butter, or coconut oil

2 cloves garlic, minced

½ medium yellow onion, chopped

½ teaspoon minced fresh ginger

1 tablespoon coconut aminos

1 tablespoon red curry paste

1 (14-ounce) can full-fat coconut milk

½ teaspoon red pepper flakes

½ teaspoon fine sea salt

¼ cup chopped cashews, for garnish

chopped fresh cilantro, for garnish

Tasty tip: Ground pork seasoned with a little bit of red pepper flakes would be delicious in this soup!

1. Preheat the oven to 400°F.

2. Cut the squash in half lengthwise. Place it cut side down on a baking sheet and bake for 30 to 35 minutes, until the squash is soft to the touch. Scoop out and discard the seeds, then scoop out the soft flesh and set aside.

3. In a large, heavy-bottomed saucepan over medium heat, combine the ghee, garlic, onion, and ginger. Cook until the onion is translucent, about 3 minutes.

4. Add the squash, coconut aminos, curry paste, coconut milk, red pepper flakes, and salt. Mix together and cook for 5 minutes, then use an immersion blender to puree the soup until smooth.

5. In a small saucepan over medium heat, toast the cashews until browned and fragrant, about 5 to 7 minutes. Make sure to move them around continuously to keep them from burning.

6. Serve the soup garnished with the cashews and cilantro.

Pineapple Sweet-and-Sour Pork Meatball Skewers (page 134)

Sweet & Crunchy Green Beans (page 198)

Hoisin Salmon (page 152)

You may also like:

winter squash
salad

Serves: 2
Prep time: 15 minutes
Cook time: 15 minutes

I won't say it again, but . . . okay, I will. I hate salads. But add caramelized squash to my salad and *I'm SO in.* Carbs are my favorite. Right after protein and fat.

4 tablespoons butter, ghee, or coconut oil, divided

1½ cups peeled and diced butternut squash (about ½ medium squash)

½ large yellow onion, thinly sliced

½ teaspoon fine sea salt, divided

1 batch Maple Mustard Vinaigrette (below)

6 cups mixed greens

2 cups cooked, pulled chicken (I used rotisserie chicken)

¼ cup sliced almonds

2 ounces crumbled goat cheese (optional)

1. In a small sauté pan over medium-low heat, combine 2 tablespoons of the butter with the butternut squash. Place the remaining 2 tablespoons of butter and the sliced onion in another small or medium sauté pan over medium-low heat. Sprinkle ¼ teaspoon of salt on the squash and ¼ teaspoon on the onion. Cook both for about 10 to 15 minutes, until the squash is soft and caramelized, tossing every couple minutes to keep everything from burning.

2. While the vegetables cook, make the vinaigrette.

3. Arrange the salad: Place the greens in a large bowl and add as much dressing as you like. Toss to coat the greens in the dressing. Add some greens to each plate, then top with the squash, onion, chicken, almonds, and goat cheese, if using. Serve immediately.

maple mustard vinaigrette (makes 1 cup)

¼ cup plus 2 tablespoons olive oil

2 tablespoons maple syrup

2 tablespoons balsamic vinegar

1 tablespoon Dijon mustard

1 tablespoon whole-grain mustard

1 clove garlic, chopped

⅛ teaspoon fine sea salt

⅛ teaspoon black pepper

1. Place all the ingredients in a blender and process until smooth. Put in the refrigerator to cool before using.

2. Store the vinaigrette in a closed container in the fridge for up to 1 week.

Tasty tips:

- If you don't feel like caramelizing onions that day, try my Overnight Slow Cooker Caramelized Onions on page 279.

- Try using sweet potato or acorn squash instead of butternut squash to mix it up!

thai coconut
chicken salad

Serves: 2

Prep time: 10 minutes

Cook time: 15 minutes

Please understand something: *I hate salads.* The only good things about a salad are the meat and the dressing. So I usually pick off all the meat and dip it in the dressing. Therefore, it's not actually a salad. But then I had a salad at Mod Market that was so good, I said to myself, okay, maybe I can do this salad thing. I can't say that this copycat salad is better, I can't say that it's worse, but it's definitely better. Just kidding, Mod Market—you're the best!

4 tablespoons coconut oil, butter, or ghee, divided

½ pound boneless, skinless chicken breast, pounded thin

¼ teaspoon fine sea salt

¼ teaspoon garlic powder

pinch of black pepper

1 small sweet potato or yam, shredded (about 2 cups)

1 batch Thai "Peanut" Dressing (below)

6 to 8 cups mixed greens

1 cucumber, diced

¼ cup unsweetened shredded coconut

roughly chopped cilantro, for garnish

1. In a large sauté pan over medium heat, melt 2 tablespoons of the coconut oil. Season the chicken on both sides with the salt, garlic powder, and pepper, then place in the hot pan. Cook for 3 to 4 minutes per side, depending on thickness, until the chicken is cooked through and no pink remains.

2. While the chicken cooks, place the remaining 2 tablespoons of coconut oil in a small sauté pan over medium heat. Add the shredded sweet potato and a bit of salt and pepper and sauté for about 5 minutes, until soft.

3. When the chicken is done, let it rest for 3 minutes, then slice it at an angle into strips.

4. Arrange the salad: Place the greens in a large bowl, add as much dressing as you like, and toss to coat. Add some greens to each plate, then top with the chicken strips, sautéed sweet potato, cucumber, coconut, and cilantro. Serve immediately.

thai "peanut" dressing (makes ⅓ cup)

¼ cup sunflower seed butter

2 tablespoons honey

2 tablespoons olive oil

2 tablespoons chopped fresh cilantro

1 tablespoon coconut vinegar

1 tablespoon coconut aminos

juice of ½ lime (about 1 tablespoon)

2 cloves garlic, chopped

1 teaspoon minced fresh ginger

½ teaspoon fine sea salt

½ teaspoon red pepper flakes

1. Place all the ingredients in a food processor or blender and process until smooth. Put in the refrigerator to cool before using.

2. Store the dressing in a closed container in the fridge for up to 1 week.

pulled pork salad
with tomatillo ranch dressing

Serves: 4

Prep time: 10 minutes

Cook time: 6 to 8 hours

The only way I really love a salad is if it's covered with lots of meat and lots of dressing. And let's not beat around the bush: Any sort of ranch is dreamy when it comes to lettuce (and pizza). Probably because it covers up the fact that you are eating leaves and acting like you enjoy it. I remember when I first began playing around with dieting at age 14 or 15 and trying to eat salads because that's what the adults did. I think that's why I hate salads so much: because they remind me of dieting, and I sure as hell don't want to diet ever again. *This salad isn't about dieting. It's about eating something delicious and feeling good afterward.* And this tomatillo ranch dressing will rock your world and your leaf-eating mouth. I promise you.

1 (2-pound) boneless pork butt or shoulder

3 cloves garlic

1 cup vegetable broth

fine sea salt

10 cups mixed greens

½ red onion, thinly sliced

1 red bell pepper, chopped

1 avocado, thinly sliced

1 batch Tomatillo Ranch Dressing (below)

lime slices, to garnish

1 Slice 3 small holes in the pork and press the garlic cloves into the holes. Place the pork in a slow cooker. Pour in the broth, then sprinkle the top of the pork generously with salt. Cover and cook on low for 6 to 8 hours, until fork-tender. Shred the meat with 2 forks and keep warm over low heat.

2 Once the pork is done, make the salad: Toss together the greens, onion, bell pepper, avocado, shredded pork, and tomatillo ranch dressing. Serve immediately with lime slices to garnish.

tomatillo ranch dressing (makes 1 cup)

1 batch Ranch Dressing (page 272)

2 tomatillos, husked and roughly chopped

¼ cup fresh cilantro, roughly chopped

1 clove garlic

1 jalapeño, roughly chopped (remove seeds for less heat)

1 Place the plain ranch dressing in a blender along with the rest of the ingredients. Blend until completely combined and smooth.

2 Store the dressing in a closed container in the refrigerator for up to 1 week.

pico de gallo
salad

Serves: 4
Prep time: 10 minutes

● ● ● ●

Pico de gallo is usually scooped up on a tortilla chip, but since we don't eat tortilla chips here in the Paleo world (well, I do sometimes . . . shhhhh), think of this as pico de gallo in giant form *. . . that you eat with a fork.* Can ya dig it?

5 plum tomatoes, cut into chunks
½ large red onion, chopped
½ jalapeño, seeded and minced
1 clove garlic, minced
juice of 2 limes (about ¼ cup)
⅓ cup chopped fresh cilantro
2 teaspoons olive oil
½ teaspoon fine sea salt

1. Place all the ingredients in a large bowl and toss to thoroughly combine.

2. The salad can be served immediately, but will get even better over time if stored in a closed container in the fridge.

Eat this salad with:

Spicy Stuffed Plantains (page 110)

Mexican Meatloaf (page 106)

Steak Frites with Herb Roasted Garlic Butter (page 114)

rosemary bacon brussels sprouts
& apple salad

Serves: 4 to 5

Prep time: 15 minutes

Cook time: 30 to 35 minutes

1 pound Brussels sprouts, ends cut off, sliced in half

3 to 4 tablespoons melted butter, ghee, or coconut oil

½ teaspoon fine sea salt

½ pound thick-cut bacon

1 large tart apple (such as Pink Lady), cored and diced

for the candied walnuts:

1 tablespoon butter, ghee, or coconut oil

2 tablespoons coconut sugar

¼ cup chopped walnuts

1 teaspoon minced fresh rosemary

pinch of fine sea salt and black pepper

Why are Brussels sprouts so hated on? Who gave them such a bad rap? *Because I'd like to smack that human across the face.* Brussels sprouts are delicious if you cook them up right! No boiling these babies. Roast 'em, pair 'em with some fruit, and sprinkle in the bacon. I'm sure there are about a million different ways to make Brussels sprouts, but I'm sticking with what I know. And what I know is that I want to be eating this right now.

1. Preheat the oven to 400°F. Line a baking sheet with parchment paper.

2. Toss the halved Brussels sprouts in the melted butter, spread out evenly on the lined baking sheet, and sprinkle with the salt. Roast for 30 to 35 minutes, until crispy.

3. While the Brussels sprouts are roasting, cook the bacon in a large sauté pan over medium heat until crispy, about 10 minutes. Remove from the pan, set aside to cool, and then chop into small pieces.

4. In the same pan, sauté the diced apple in the bacon fat until soft. Remove from the heat and set aside.

5. Make the candied walnuts: Melt the butter in a small saucepan over medium heat. Add the coconut sugar and walnuts and toss to coat for about 2 minutes.

6. Place the pan with the apples back over medium heat. Add the candied walnuts, roasted Brussels sprouts, bacon, and rosemary, season with a bit of salt and pepper, and then mix to incorporate. Serve immediately.

Maple Vanilla Candied Walnuts (page 210)

Sweet & Crunchy Green Beans (page 198)

Honey Thyme Roasted Acorn Squash (page 188)

You may also like:

oven
parsnip fries

Serves: 2 to 3

Prep time: 5 minutes, plus time to make the aioli, if desired

Cook time: 35 minutes

● ● ● ●

I think pretty much everyone connects with a good French fry. I personally was raised on fries because I refused to eat anything else. Oh yeah, duh, and donuts. Love those things. But fries are one of those foods that are hard to say goodbye to when starting Paleo. And since so many restaurants use canola oil for frying, they are just something that is better to make at home. *These fries are crunchy on the outside but soft on the inside,* so they hold up great when dunked in a little Truffle Aioli (page 275).

3 large parsnips, ends removed, peeled

3 tablespoons melted coconut oil or butter

½ teaspoon fine sea salt

¼ teaspoon garlic powder

1 batch Truffle Aioli (page 275; optional)

1. Preheat the oven to 375°F. Line a baking sheet with parchment paper.

2. Cut the peeled parsnips into your preferred French fry shapes. I like to cut them in half lengthwise, then make strips and cut those strips into French fry lengths.

3. Toss the fries in the melted coconut oil, then sprinkle the salt and garlic powder over the fries and toss once more until coated.

4. Place the fries on the lined baking sheet, making sure they don't overlap. Bake for 25 minutes, until slightly soft but crispy on the bottom.

5. Remove from the oven and toss (the fries will brown more on the bottom than on the top). Turn up the oven temperature to 500°F, then bake for 8 to 10 more minutes, until the fries are crispy. Keep an eye on them to make sure they don't burn.

6. Serve hot, with Truffle Aioli on the side for dipping, if desired.

Eat these fries with:

Steak Frites with Herb Roasted Garlic Butter (page 114)

Truffle Mushroom Burgers (page 112)

Fall-Off-the-Bone Slow Cooker Baby Back Ribs (page 126)

spicy
sweet potatoes

Serves: 4

Prep time: 10 minutes

Cook time: 30 minutes

Here's the thing: People will fight all day long about the difference between sweet potatoes and yams. I absolutely, positively do not care what the difference is. They both taste sweet and delicious. So eat whichever you want, sweet potato or yam; *just eat them baked like this,* which may turn into your new favorite recipe.

2 medium sweet potatoes

2 teaspoons fine sea salt

1 teaspoon garlic powder

1 teaspoon paprika

¼ teaspoon chili powder

¼ teaspoon ground cumin

¼ teaspoon cayenne pepper

¼ cup melted butter, ghee, or coconut oil

1. Preheat the oven to 400°F and line a baking sheet with parchment paper.

2. Wash and scrub the sweet potatoes, then dice into 1-inch pieces.

3. In a large bowl, combine the salt and spices, then place the sweet potatoes on top. Pour the melted butter over the sweet potatoes and toss to coat.

4. Place the sweet potatoes on the parchment-lined baking sheet and bake for 30 minutes, until fork-tender. Serve immediately.

Tasty tip:
Try these in a hash with eggs, peppers, and onions.

You may also like:

Breakfast Baked Sweet Potatoes (page 58)

Sweet Potato Waffles (page 54)

Rosemary Roasted Beets (page 192)

honey thyme
roasted acorn squash

Serves: 4

Prep time: 10 minutes

Cook time: 30 to 40 minutes

● ● ● ●

For me, this dish screams holiday food. Doesn't it just look like it should be on your holiday table, right next to everything else rich and decadent? Well, you don't want to wait for the holidays to make this dish. *And you won't feel guilty after eating it all!*

1 large acorn squash

2 tablespoons melted butter, ghee, or coconut oil

½ teaspoon fine sea salt

¼ cup pecans, chopped

¼ cup walnuts, chopped

3 tablespoons honey

1 tablespoon butter, ghee, or coconut oil

2 tablespoons fresh thyme, minced

pinch of fine sea salt

Tasty tip:
Try this recipe with butternut squash, sweet potatoes, or pumpkin.

1. Preheat the oven to 400°F. Line a baking sheet with parchment paper.

2. Cut the squash in half lengthwise and scoop out the seeds with a spoon. Cut the squash down the grooves to create 6 to 8 half-moons. Place each half-moon on the lined baking sheet.

3. Use a brush to wipe each half-moon with the melted butter. Sprinkle with the salt.

4. Bake for 30 to 40 minutes, until the squash is soft and caramelized.

5. While the squash is baking, toast the pecans and walnuts in a small sauté pan until slightly browned and fragrant. Add the honey, 1 tablespoon of butter, thyme, and salt and mix until the butter has melted.

6. When the squash is done, pour some of the nut mixture into the middle of each half-moon and serve immediately.

Pistachio Rosemary Lamb Chops (page 144)

Creamy Apple Sage Brined Pork Chops (page 132)

Chicken Carbonara Casserole (page 94)

Eat this dish alongside:

lemon truffle
roasted cauliflower

Serves: 4

Prep time: 5 minutes

Cook time: 25 minutes

Raw cauliflower smells like farts. I hate it raw. I remember watching this guy in my college dorm cafeteria eat a bowl of raw broccoli and cauliflower every day for lunch, and I couldn't fathom how he did that. It must have been miserable to eat. Especially without ranch. But when I found out how delicious cauliflower is when you cook it, I started eating it almost every day. Don't eat cauliflower raw; it should be against the law.

1 head cauliflower, cut into florets

3 tablespoons melted ghee or butter

2 teaspoons lemon juice

1 teaspoon white truffle oil

1 teaspoon fine sea salt

¼ teaspoon black pepper

for garnish:

chopped fresh parsley

coarse sea salt

1. Preheat the oven to 400°F. Line a baking sheet with parchment paper.

2. Toss the cauliflower florets in the ghee, lemon juice, truffle oil, salt, and pepper.

3. Spread the cauliflower on the lined baking sheet and bake for 15 minutes. Turn with a spatula, then bake for 10 more minutes, until the cauliflower is fork-tender and slightly browned.

4. Serve immediately, garnished with chopped parsley and coarse sea salt.

Pair this dish with:

Steak Frites with Herb Roasted Garlic Butter, minus the frites (page 114)

Pork & Artichoke Stuffed Portabella Mushrooms (page 140)

Turkey Meatballs (page 96)

rosemary roasted
beets

Serves: 4

Prep time: 10 minutes

Cook time: 50 to 55 minutes

Don't be scared when your pee has a hint of red to it after you eat these beets. *You're not dying.*

3 cups diced beets

¼ cup melted butter, ghee, or coconut oil

1 tablespoon minced fresh rosemary

1 teaspoon coarse sea salt

1. Preheat the oven to 400°F. Line a baking sheet with parchment paper.

2. Toss the beets in the melted butter and sprinkle with the rosemary and coarse sea salt.

3. Place the beets on the lined baking sheet and roast for 50 to 55 minutes, until crispy on the outside and soft on the inside. Serve immediately.

Tasty tip:
For a different spin on delicious beets, try roasting the beets in balsamic vinegar and then tossing them with some toasted walnuts!

Eat this dish with:

Steak Frites with Herb Roasted Garlic Butter (page 114)

Maple Bacon Pork Loin (page 128)

White Wine Butter Scallops (page 160)

crispy smoked
paprika radishes

Serves: 4

Prep time: 5 minutes

Cook time: 30 to 35 minutes

I don't like radishes in the raw. Nah, man. But baked radishes remind me of potatoes. *And I love me some potatoes.*

2 large bunches radishes, halved

1 small sweet onion, cut into large chunks

¼ cup melted butter, ghee, or coconut oil

1 teaspoon smoked paprika

1 teaspoon fine sea salt

½ teaspoon cayenne pepper

pinch of black pepper

1. Preheat the oven to 400°F. Line a baking sheet with parchment paper.

2. Toss the radishes and onion in the melted butter, then coat with the paprika, salt, cayenne pepper, and black pepper.

3. Spread out evenly on the lined baking sheet and bake for 30 to 35 minutes, until the radishes are crispy on the outside and soft on the inside. Serve immediately.

You may also like:

Spicy Sweet Potatoes (page 186)

Mexican Meatloaf (page 106)

Spicy Stuffed Plantains (page 110)

oven-roasted
fennel

Serves: 4

Prep time: 10 minutes

Cook time: 30 minutes

● ● ● ●

3 medium fennel bulbs

3 to 4 tablespoons melted butter, ghee, or coconut oil

1 teaspoon garlic powder

1 teaspoon fine sea salt

The first time I had fennel was at Bill and Hayley's house in Pittsburgh. They caramelized it with some coconut aminos, and I couldn't get enough of it. I was too scared to make it on my own because I didn't want to screw it up, until I saw Ina Garten on the Food Network smoothly roast fennel in a snap. *This is me trying to be Ina Garten.* Now I just need a beach house in the Hamptons where I can throw outdoor parties with cheese plates.

1. Preheat the oven to 400°F. Line a baking sheet with parchment paper.

2. Trim the fennel stalks just above the bulbs. Slice each bulb thinly from top to bottom.

3. Place the fennel slices on the lined baking sheet and pour the melted butter on top, tossing to coat. Sprinkle with the garlic powder and salt.

4. Roast for 30 minutes, until soft and golden brown. Serve immediately.

Roast more veggies:

Crispy Smoked Paprika Radishes (page 194)

Lemon Truffle Roasted Cauliflower (page 190)

Spicy Sweet Potatoes (page 186)

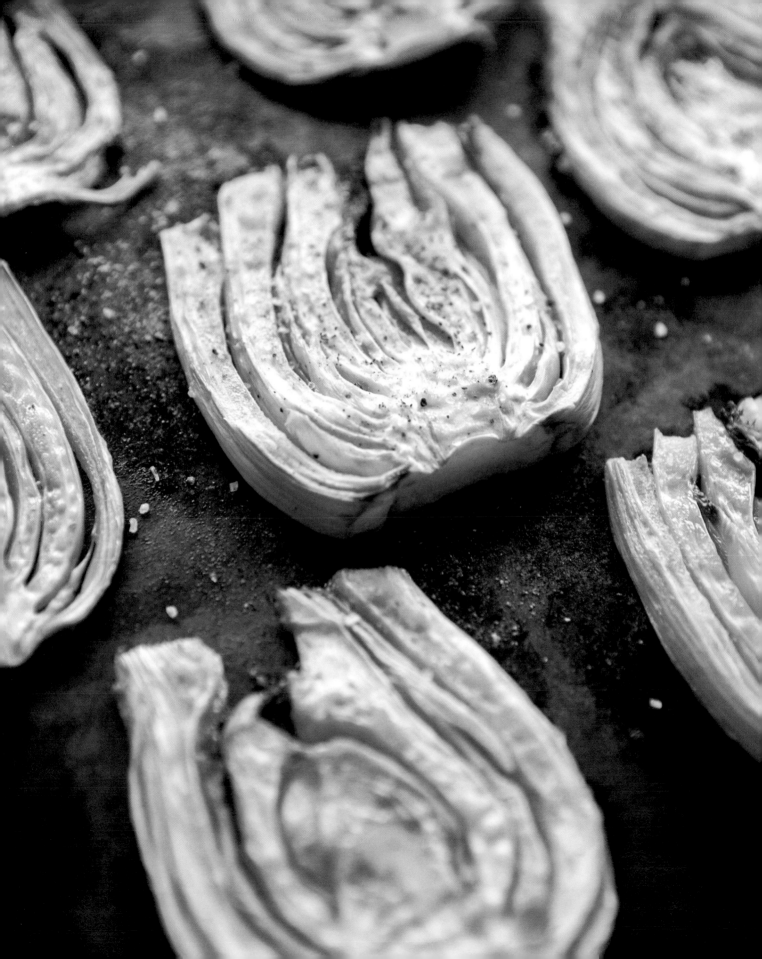

sweet & crunchy
green beans

Serves: 4

Prep time: 10 minutes

Cook time: 45 minutes

I eat green beans once a year. At Thanksgiving. Honestly, they rarely make an appearance in my kitchen. I don't know why, because they are beautiful and extremely tasty. Add a little butter and salt and BOOM, you have a delicious side dish. *But I turned it up a notch.* Just for you. Now you have sweet AND salty. BOOM BOOM is what I like to say.

1 pound green beans, ends trimmed

½ pound thick-cut bacon

½ medium yellow onion, chopped

½ cup coconut aminos

¼ cup sliced almonds

1 Bring a large stockpot of water to a boil. Add the green beans and cook for 10 minutes, until crisp-tender. Drain the beans and place them in a bowl of ice water to preserve their color.

2 In a large sauté pan over medium heat, cook the bacon until crispy, about 10 minutes. Remove from the pan and set aside to cool, then chop into small pieces.

3 Leave 3 tablespoons of bacon fat in the pan and reserve the rest for another use. Add the onion and sauté until translucent, about 7 minutes.

4 Add the coconut aminos to the pan with the onion. Cook over medium-low heat until the mixture reduces and coats the back of a spoon, about 10 minutes.

5 Add the green beans, toss, and cook for 5 minutes, until warmed through.

6 Pour the green bean mixture into a large bowl, add the almonds, and toss to combine. Serve immediately.

Eat this dish with:

Fall-Off-the-Bone Slow Cooker Baby Back Ribs (page 126)

Maple Bacon Pork Loin (page 128)

Steak Frites with Herb Roasted Garlic Butter (page 114)

cauliflower rice
five ways

Serves: 4

Prep time: 10 minutes, plus time to make the pesto, if using

Cook time: 8 to 12 minutes

Cauliflower rice has been my saving grace when it comes to Paleo. I still eat white rice when I feel like it since it doesn't mess with my stomach too much and I work out on a regular basis, but I try not to go overboard. Cauliflower rice is an amazing substitute that is surprisingly filling. Once you begin to make cauliflower rice, you will find yourself wanting it more and more. *Guilt-free satisfaction right there.*

1 head cauliflower, chopped into florets

3 tablespoons butter, ghee, or coconut oil

½ teaspoon garlic powder

½ teaspoon fine sea salt

for cilantro lime rice:

¼ cup fresh cilantro, minced

juice of ½ lime (about 1 tablespoon)

for mexican-style rice:

1 (8-ounce) can tomato sauce

2 plum tomatoes, diced

¼ teaspoon chili powder

¼ teaspoon ground cumin

3 tablespoons minced fresh cilantro

for pesto rice:

1 to 2 tablespoons Dairy-Free Pesto (page 280)

for quick fried rice:

1 tablespoon butter, ghee, or coconut oil

2 eggs, whisked

2 tablespoons coconut aminos

½ teaspoon fish sauce

1 small carrot, shredded

2 scallions, minced

1. Rice the cauliflower. There are two ways to do it: either grate the florets into a large bowl using a cheese grater, or run the florets through a food processor using the regular blade or, even better, the shredding attachment.

2. In a large sauté pan over medium heat, combine the butter and riced cauliflower. Sprinkle with the garlic powder and salt and mix well. Cook for 8 to 10 minutes, until the cauliflower is soft, moving it around every couple minutes to keep it from browning/burning on the bottom. If you want plain cauliflower rice, you're done. For flavored rice, see below.

3. **For cilantro lime rice:** Add the cilantro and lime juice to the pan with the cooked rice and cook for 1 to 2 more minutes to combine and heat through.

4. **For Mexican-style rice:** Add the tomato sauce, tomatoes, chili powder, and cumin to the pan with the cooked rice and cook for 1 to 2 more minutes to combine and heat through. Fold in the cilantro before serving.

5. **For pesto rice:** Add the pesto to the pan with the cooked rice and cook for 1 to 2 more minutes to combine and heat through.

6. **For quick fried rice:** Remove the cooked rice from the pan and set it aside. Add the butter to the pan, then the eggs, and cook until scrambled. Set the cooked eggs aside. Return the cauliflower rice to the pan, then add the coconut aminos, fish sauce, and carrot and mix well. Fold in the scrambled eggs and scallions and mix well to incorporate.

cauliflower puree

Serves: 3

Prep time: 20 minutes

Cook time: 15 minutes

● ● ● ●

Since white potatoes fall into the "gray area" of Paleo foods (see page 26), I have been substituting cauliflower for potatoes for years. Personally, I'm going to eat potatoes when I want potatoes. I don't give a crap. BUT, if you are looking for a lower-carb substitute, this cauliflower puree is where it's at. *It's rich, creamy, and hearty,* and you'll be surprised at how fast it fills you up! Eat it; just do it.

1 head cauliflower, chopped into florets

½ teaspoon garlic powder

½ teaspoon fine sea salt

chopped fresh chives, for garnish (optional)

1. Steam the cauliflower until fork-tender, about 15 minutes.

2. Transfer the steamed cauliflower to a blender or food processor and puree until smooth. It should resemble mashed potatoes. Add the garlic powder and salt and puree once more.

3. Serve garnished with chopped fresh chives, if desired.

Tip:
If you use a high-speed blender such as a Blendtec, getting the right consistency is rather easy. If you use another type of blender or a food processor, you may have to add a bit of coconut milk or water to get a creamy consistency.

This puree goes great with:

Pistachio Rosemary Lamb Chops (page 144)

Rich & Hearty Bacon Beef Stew (page 120)

Turkey Meatballs (page 96)

snacks

Snack like you give a damn.

When it comes to snacking, I go through spurts. Sometimes I'll just eat three meals a day and I'm totally fine. Other times I'll eat every hour, on the hour—like right now, while I'm putting together this cookbook. My body changes from year to year, and my eating habits change along with it.

Snacks always seem to be the hardest foods for people to give up when they transition to Paleo. Before going Paleo, many of us would eat little cracker snack packs or a protein bar or even a Snickers bar. For me, snacks filled 90 percent of my diet before Paleo because they were so easy to come by. You can find them anywhere. But with Paleo, you have to plan a bit more. *Remember, failing to plan is planning to fail.* Just pure fact.

bacon buffalo
deviled eggs

Yield: 1 dozen

Prep time: 10 minutes, plus time to make the mayo and 10 to 15 minutes to chill

Cook time: 15 minutes

I've made so many deviled eggs on my blog. Because the possibilities are endless. *If you are trying to figure out more things to snack on, deviled eggs are the perfect solution.* They are loaded with protein and fat and will keep you fuller, longer. I just solved any snacking issue you've ever had. Boom.

6 large eggs

2 slices bacon

¼ cup Super Simple Mayonnaise (page 274)

¼ cup hot sauce (I prefer Tessemae's or Frank's RedHot)

¼ teaspoon garlic powder

⅛ teaspoon fine sea salt

⅛ teaspoon black pepper

½ medium carrot, minced

½ stalk celery, minced

chopped fresh chives, for garnish

1. Bring a large pot of water to a boil. Use a ladle to gentle immerse the eggs in the boiling water. Cook for 15 minutes, then place the cooked eggs in a bowl of ice water to cool.

2. While the eggs are cooking, cook the bacon in a sauté pan over medium heat until crispy, about 10 minutes. Let cool, then chop into small pieces.

3. Once the eggs have cooled, peel them, cut them in half, and scoop out the yolks. Place the yolks in a food processor and pulse to break them up.

4. Add the mayo, hot sauce, garlic powder, salt, and pepper to the food processor and puree until smooth. Place the pureed yolk mixture in a bowl and mix with most of the bacon pieces, reserving some for garnish.

5. Transfer the yolk mixture to a small resealable plastic bag, cut off one corner of the bag, and squeeze the mixture into the egg white halves. Chill for 10 to 15 minutes, then garnish with the reserved bacon pieces, carrot, celery, and chives.

Want more eggs?

Breakfast Baked Sweet Potatoes (page 58)

Individual Breakfast Pizzas (page 64)

Breakfast Tacos (page 70)

sweet & spicy
sesame almonds

Serves: 6 to 8

Prep time: 5 minutes

Cook time: 15 minutes

If you like football, unlike me, you should make these for one or all of your football parties. *I would actually come to that party* if I knew these almonds were involved.

½ cup maple syrup

2 tablespoons chili sauce

1 (1-inch) piece of fresh ginger, finely grated

2 cups raw almonds

1 tablespoon sesame seeds

1 Preheat the oven to 350°F. Line a rimmed baking sheet with parchment paper.

2 In a small bowl, whisk together the maple syrup, chili sauce, and ginger until well combined. Add the almonds and toss to coat in the mixture.

3 Pour the coated almonds onto the lined baking sheet and spread them out evenly. Bake for 15 minutes, tossing every 5 minutes to ensure that they cook evenly. At the 15-minute mark, the almonds should be fragrant and slightly browned, but not burned.

4 Remove from the oven and immediately sprinkle the hot almonds with the sesame seeds. Let cool for 5 to 10 minutes before serving.

Tasty tip:
Other ways to spice up almonds:

- With rosemary
- With thyme
- With cinnamon and cocoa powder
- With honey and cinnamon
- With chai spices and maple syrup

Try more crunchy things:

Maple Vanilla Candied Walnuts (page 210)

Tostones (page 212)

Coffee Caramel Chocolate Almond Bark (page 220)

maple vanilla
candied walnuts

Serves: 6 to 8

Prep time: 5 minutes

Cook time: 20 minutes

I once had a friend who babysat some kids whose parents owned a candied nuts stand. Still with me? Well, I spent most of my senior year of high school eating candied walnuts, pecans, almonds, and whatever else they gave me. *I ate so many candied nuts that by the end of my senior year, I had ripped four pairs of jeans.* I blamed it on puberty or hormones, but I can face the truth now. So remember, life is about keeping things in moderation, candied nuts included. And stretchy pants.

2 cups raw walnuts

⅓ cup maple syrup

1 teaspoon vanilla extract

pinch of fine sea salt

½ cup coconut sugar

¼ teaspoon ground cinnamon

1. Preheat the oven to 350°F. Line a baking sheet with parchment paper.

2. In a large bowl, toss the walnuts, maple syrup, vanilla extract, and salt. Pour the coated walnuts onto the lined baking sheet and spread them out evenly.

3. Bake for 20 minutes, turning the nuts every 5 minutes to keep them from burning. After 20 minutes, the walnuts should be fragrant and golden brown.

4. While the nuts are roasting, mix together the coconut sugar and cinnamon in a large bowl.

5. Add the roasted walnuts to the bowl with the coconut sugar mixture and toss until well coated. Spread out on the baking sheet and let cool before eating.

Treat yo'self:

Coffee Caramel Chocolate Almond Bark (page 220)

"Peanut Butter" & Jelly Cups (page 218)

Buckeyes (page 222)

tostones
(fried green plantains)

Serves: 4
Prep time: 10 minutes
Cook time: 16 minutes

2 green plantains
¼ to ½ cup coconut oil
1 teaspoon coarse sea salt

I told you I would have more plantain recipes for you. And now you can see my favorites. I personally enjoy maduros (page 214) more than tostones because maduros are sweeter, but both are divine. *Think of tostones just like chips:* dip them, snack on them, or even add meat, like Carne Mechada (page 122), to the playing field, and whoaaaaa doggy, you have my attention.

1. Cut the ends off the plantains, peel them, and cut them into 1-inch-thick discs.

2. Place ¼ to ½ cup of coconut oil in a small sauté pan over medium heat. You need enough fat to cover the plantains about halfway, so the exact amount will depend on the size of your pan. Once the oil is hot (water sizzles on top when added), add the plantains and cook for 3 to 5 minutes per side, until browned and slightly soft. You may need to cook them in batches to avoid overcrowding the pan. Place the cooked plantains on a paper towel to drain the excess oil. Turn down the heat to medium-low since the oil will be used once more.

3. Place the plantains on a cutting board, then use the bottom of a drinking glass or soup can or a mallet to flatten them to about half their thickness.

4. Turn the heat back up to medium, then place the smashed plantains back in the hot oil to fry for about 2 to 3 minutes per side, until they turn a deep golden color. Place back on the paper towel and sprinkle with the coarse sea salt before serving.

You may also like:

Guasacaca (page 286)

Spicy Stuffed Plantains (page 110)

Lechón Asado (page 138)

maduros
(fried sweet plantains)

Serves: 4

Prep time: 5 minutes

Cook time: 10 to 12 minutes

Be still my heart. These sweet fried plantains are what make life worth living. After plantains turn soft and brown, they become sweeter and way tastier than before. Once you fry them to get a beautiful brown crust, you will swoon over plantains and the way they melt in your mouth. *Can you tell that I go a bit gaga over plantains?* Eat them as a side dish with a salty meat or as a starchy post-workout snack. Either way, you will fall in love with maduros and be searching for plantains on a weekly basis!

2 very ripe brown plantains (get the softest ones you can find)

¼ to ½ cup coconut oil

pinch of fine sea salt

1. Cut the ends off the plantains, peel them, and cut them on the diagonal into 1-inch-thick slices.

2. Place ¼ to ½ cup of coconut oil in a small sauté pan over medium heat. You need enough fat to cover the plantains about halfway, so the exact amount will depend on the size of your pan. Once the oil is hot (water sizzles on top when added), add the plantains and cook for about 2 minutes per side, until golden brown. You may need to cook them in batches to avoid overcrowding the pan.

3. Reduce the heat to low and keep cooking, turning every minute until the plantains have caramelized, about 4 to 6 minutes. Place on a paper towel to soak up the excess oil, and sprinkle with a pinch of salt before serving.

Try eating maduros with:

Chimichurri (page 284) on top

Guasacaca (page 286) on the side

Eggs and bacon topped with hollandaise (page 276)

desserts

A sweet for my sweet.

When I first started Paleo, desserts were very exciting to me. I felt like I had just signed my name on the dotted line stating that I would never eat crap food again, but *I found myself eating a jar of almond butter* or stuffing chocolate chips into dates (the dried fruit kind, not the human kind). It took me a while to admit to myself that life is about moderation. And that includes Paleo desserts. Just because something doesn't have gluten or grains in it doesn't mean that you should be consuming it at every meal or in mass quantities.

Dessert is something I will never give up. I tried, and it did not go over well. I have to have balance in all parts of my life. So if I'm craving dessert, I will have it. Over time I've learned to listen to my body and stop eating before I'm uncomfortably full. That goes for breakfast, lunch, snack, dinner, and dessert. Moderation is key to a healthy and sustainable lifestyle. There's my two cents. Take it or leave it. But you should probably take it, because I'm right 124 percent of the time. Minus 100 percent.

"peanut butter"
& jelly cups

Yield: 9 cups

Prep time: 10 minutes, plus time to make the jam and 25 minutes to freeze

● ● ● ●

2 cups dark chocolate chips

¼ cup sunflower seed butter

2 tablespoons honey, melted if needed

¼ cup Raspberry-Strawberry Jam (page 294)

coarse sea salt, for garnish

I don't really miss the foods I have given up. Like bread. What I do think about regularly, though, is peanut butter and jelly. *Those two were made for each other.* Like Ross and Rachel. Or margaritas and lime. Or CrossFit and Paleo (ugh, sorry to be THAT person). And since I don't really feel like making a loaf of bread, I'll just put the peanut butter and jelly in chocolate instead. Genius, if you ask me.

1. Place 9 paper liners in a muffin tin.

2. Melt the chocolate in a double boiler or in a bowl in the microwave.

3. Place less than 1 tablespoon of melted chocolate in each muffin liner, spreading the chocolate over the bottom of the liner and up the sides.

4. Place the muffin tin in the freezer for at least 5 minutes, until the chocolate is frozen solid.

5. While the chocolate freezes, mix together the sunflower seed butter and honey.

6. When the chocolate in the muffin cups has frozen, remove the muffin tin from the freezer. Place a little over 1 teaspoon of the sunflower seed butter mixture in the middle of each cup, pressing down to flatten it out and making sure that chocolate can still be seen around the edge.

7. Spread about 2 teaspoons of the jam on top of the sunflower seed butter in each cup. Place in the freezer to harden for 10 minutes.

8. Pour 1 to 2 tablespoons of the melted chocolate on top of the hardened sunflower seed butter and jam, making sure that the chocolate falls around the edge to help seal the cup. (If the chocolate has cooled to the point that it is no longer pourable, just reheat it a bit and stir to smooth it out.) Sprinkle a small pinch of coarse sea salt on top of each cup.

9. Place in the freezer for at least 10 minutes, until frozen solid. Let the chocolate cups sit at room temperature for 1 to 2 minutes before consuming so the chocolate can soften.

10. Store in a sealed container in the refrigerator for up to 2 weeks.

coffee caramel
chocolate almond bark

Yield: Fifteen 2-inch pieces

Prep time: 5 minutes, plus time to make the caramel sauce and 15 minutes to freeze

Cook time: 12 minutes

Chocolate bark is one of those *stupid simple recipes* that feels like an elaborate one. There's really nothing elaborate about it. You're melting chocolate, throwing a bunch of stuff on top of it, and freezing it. So if you want to impress your guests while giving about 10 percent effort, this dessert is your soul mate.

½ cup raw almonds

1½ cups dark chocolate chips

1 teaspoon coffee grounds (I used instant coffee grounds)

½ teaspoon vanilla extract

½ batch Vanilla Bean Caramel Sauce (page 250)

¼ teaspoon coarse sea salt

1. Preheat the oven to 350°F.

2. Place the almonds on a baking sheet and roast for 12 minutes, moving them around halfway through the cooking time so they roast evenly. Let cool, then roughly chop.

3. Melt the chocolate in a double boiler or in a bowl in the microwave. Mix in the coffee grounds and vanilla extract.

4. Line a rimmed baking sheet with parchment paper. Pour the chocolate mixture onto the baking sheet and spread it out evenly. Sprinkle the almonds on top of the chocolate, then use a spoon to drizzle the caramel sauce on top. Sprinkle with the coarse sea salt.

5. Place in the freezer for 15 minutes. Run a knife under hot water for 1 minute, then chop the bark into 2-inch pieces before serving.

6. Store in a closed container in the refrigerator for up to 2 weeks.

Tasty tip:
You have absolute freedom when it comes to this recipe. You can put whatever you want on top! Here are some ideas to help you mix and match:

Nuts: walnuts, macadamia nuts, pecans, or pistachios

Dried fruit: strawberries, blueberries, cranberries, figs, or dates

Fresh fruit: raspberries, pomegranates, blueberries, or cherries

Butters: almond butter, sunflower seed butter, cashew butter, or coconut butter

Extra goodies: coconut chips or chocolate chips

buckeyes

Yield: 18 to 20 buckeyes

Prep time: 30 minutes, plus 45 minutes to set

Now, don't get mad that I used powdered sugar in here. I just had to. You can get maple sugar pretty damn fine if you run it through a food processor for a while, but it's just not the same as powdered sugar. This is one of those desserts that should be eaten in moderation. After eating Paleo for five years now, I find that things taste much sweeter than they used to. These taste REALLY sweet, and you should be happy to eat just one. *Maybe two, if it's that time of the month.* But be careful; this can turn into sugar overload reaaaaal quick. Which ends in a sugar coma. And an unhappy sugar-loaded self.

1½ cups sunflower seed butter

½ cup (1 stick) butter, softened to room temperature

1 teaspoon vanilla extract

2 cups organic powdered sugar, divided

1½ cups dark chocolate chips

1 Place the sunflower seed butter, butter, and vanilla extract in a food processor and puree until creamy.

2 Add ½ cup of the powdered sugar and puree again, then repeat with the rest of the sugar until completely combined.

3 Use a 1½-tablespoon cookie scoop to scoop out a ball of the dough, then shape it in your hands. Place on a plate lined with parchment paper. Repeat until you have made 18 to 20 balls.

4 Place the balls in the freezer for about 30 minutes, until hard.

5 Melt the chocolate in a double boiler or in a bowl in the microwave. Use a toothpick to dip each ball into the melted chocolate, then place it back on the parchment paper.

6 Refrigerate the dipped balls for 10 to 15 minutes, until the chocolate has set.

More chocolate, please:

Coffee Caramel Chocolate Almond Bark (page 220)

"Peanut Butter" & Jelly Cups (page 218)

"Peanut Butter" Cream Pie (page 236)

two-toned
chewy cookies

Yield: 10 cookies

Prep time: 10 minutes

Cook time: 10 minutes

These double chewy chocolate cookies are based on the most popular cookie recipe on my website. These were inspired by a simple peanut butter cookie I had once growing up. They are stupid easy and stupid delicious. It's all just so stupid. And these are two-toned. If that's not creativity, I don't know what is. (I'm being sarcastic here, if you didn't get my drift. Come on, get with it!)

1 cup thick almond butter (I prefer the Maranatha brand or freshly ground almond butter)

1 cup coconut sugar

1 large egg, whisked

1 teaspoon baking soda

1 teaspoon vanilla extract

pinch of fine sea salt

¼ to ½ cup dark chocolate chips, depending on how chocolaty you want your cookies

¼ cup unsweetened cocoa powder

1. Preheat the oven to 350°F. Line a baking sheet with parchment paper.

2. In a large bowl, mix together the almond butter and coconut sugar using a large wooden spoon. Add the egg and mix until well combined.

3. Add the baking soda, vanilla extract, and salt and mix until everything is well combined. Then fold in the chocolate chips. This is all hands for me—hands are just better than spoons, everyone knows that.

4. Form the dough into a ball and divide it in half. Place half of the dough on a plate. To the remaining dough, add the cocoa powder and mix it in with your hands until completely combined.

5. Use a 1½-tablespoon cookie scoop to scoop up some of the chocolate dough and press it into one half of the scoop. Then scoop up some of the vanilla dough and press it into the other half of the scoop. Push the dough down into the scoop so it stays combined once removed, then place the ball of dough on the lined baking sheet. Repeat this process to make 10 cookies, spacing the balls of dough about 1 inch apart.

6. Use a fork to press down the balls of dough just slightly. There's no need to really flatten them out; just get them into more of a cookie shape than a ball shape.

7. Bake for 10 minutes, until the cookies are baked through. Do not overcook; they will harden a bit as they cool.

8. Let cool on the pan for 5 to 10 minutes, then transfer to a cooling rack to cool completely. Be patient, my child; you don't want these to fall apart on you!

blueberry lemon poppy seed
ice cream

Yield: 1 pint

Prep time: 15 minutes

Churn time: About 15 minutes (it depends on your ice cream maker)

Dude. Taking pictures of ice cream is one of the most stressful things ever. Okay, I tend to exaggerate. But this picture did take us multiple tries. If the ice cream is too hard, you can't make beautiful little scoops. If it's too soft, it will melt and become a sloppy mess. The moral of the story here: *Just eat the ice cream instead of trying to get a sweet Instagram pic.* #melting #awcrap #foodpicsarethebest

2 (14-ounce) cans full-fat coconut milk

½ cup lemon juice, preferably from Meyer lemons (I used 4 Meyer lemons)

grated zest of 1 lemon (about 1½ tablespoons)

¾ cup honey, divided

1 teaspoon vanilla extract

½ cup fresh or frozen blueberries

2 tablespoons poppy seeds

Tasty tip:
Try making this ice cream with different fruits, such as raspberries, strawberries, cherries, or even grapes!

1. Make the ice cream base: In a large bowl, whisk together the coconut milk, lemon juice, lemon zest, ½ cup of the honey, and vanilla extract until well combined. Set aside.

2. In a small saucepan over medium heat, combine the blueberries and the remaining ¼ cup of honey. Let come to a slow bubble, then continue to cook until the blueberries explode, about 8 to 10 minutes. Remove from the heat and set aside.

3. Right before you pour the ice cream base into the ice cream maker, whisk in the poppy seeds. Churn the mixture following the manufacturer's instructions.

4. Once the ice cream begins to thicken, about 10 minutes, pour in the cooled blueberry mixture. Continue to churn the ice cream until it stiffens.

5. Serve immediately or place in a sealed container in the freezer. If serving after storing in the freezer, you may need to let the ice cream sit out at room temperature for an hour or so before scooping and serving.

"Peanut Butter" & Jelly Cups (page 218)

"Peanut Butter" Cream Pie (page 236)

Buckeyes (page 222)

Stay cool, my friends:

caramel
apple crisp

Serves: 6

Prep time: 15 minutes, plus time to make the caramel sauce

Cook time: 25 to 30 minutes

● ● ● ●

for the apple mixture:

5 apples (I used Fuji apples)

⅓ cup coconut sugar

⅓ cup maple syrup

3 tablespoons tapioca flour/starch

2 teaspoons lemon juice

1 teaspoon ground cinnamon

⅛ teaspoon fine sea salt

for the topping:

1 cup walnuts, chopped

½ cup sliced almonds

¼ cup melted butter

⅓ cup coconut sugar

1 tablespoon tapioca flour/starch

½ teaspoon ground cinnamon

⅛ teaspoon fine sea salt

coconut milk ice cream, for serving

1 batch Vanilla Bean Caramel Sauce (page 250)

fresh mint, for garnish

Tasty tip:
Try making this crisp with other fresh fruit, such as blueberries, raspberries, or cherries.

I once went on an incredibly awful date. The guy was a total tool. BUT we ordered an apple crisp dessert that was out-of-this-world good. It was topped with caramel, candied walnuts, and ice cream. *I ate 95 percent of it to get back at him for being a jerk. I sure showed that guy.*

1. Preheat the oven to 350°F.

2. Peel, core, and dice the apples and place them in a pie pan. Add the rest of the ingredients for the apple mixture and toss to coat the apples.

3. In a small bowl, mix together the ingredients for the topping. Sprinkle the topping evenly over the coated apples. Use a spoon to drizzle half of the caramel sauce over the apple crisp mixture.

4. Bake for 25 to 30 minutes, until the nut mixture on top is golden brown.

5. Let rest for 5 to 10 minutes before serving, then use a slotted spoon (the apples will render some liquid) to scoop each serving of apple crisp. Serve with ice cream, drizzled with the remaining caramel sauce and garnished with fresh mint.

You may also like:

Maple Vanilla Candied Walnuts (page 210)

Carrot Cake Layered "Cheesecake" (page 240)

"peanut butter"
cream pie

Yield: One 10-inch pie (serving 10)

Prep time: 20 minutes, plus at least 8 hours to refrigerate the cans of coconut milk, at least 3 hours to refrigerate the pie, and time to make the whipped cream

● ● ● ●

If it weren't for Hayley, this peanut butter pie wouldn't be nearly as beautiful. She has mad skills when it comes to decorating desserts. My decorating involves plopping the whipped cream on the pie and sprinkling chocolate chips wherever they feel like going. Including the floor. Just telling you ahead of time so you understand that it doesn't have to be this beautiful. Mine absolutely won't be when I make it again. *Thanks, Hayley.* If it weren't for you, this book would look a whole lot different.

for the filling:

2 (14-ounce) cans full-fat coconut milk, refrigerated overnight

⅔ cup sunflower seed butter

¼ cup honey

1 teaspoon vanilla extract

⅛ teaspoon ground cinnamon

1 tablespoon powdered gelatin, divided

for the crust:

1 cup raw cashews

½ cup raw almonds

⅔ cup coconut sugar

¼ cup unsweetened cocoa powder

¼ cup (½ stick) butter, melted

½ teaspoon vanilla extract

pinch of fine sea salt

toppings:

1 batch Whipped Cream (page 296)

½ cup dark chocolate chips

1. Refrigerate the cans of coconut milk overnight to help the coconut cream separate from the coconut water. When you're ready to make the pie, open the cans. The coconut cream should have separated from the water and risen to the top. Scoop off the white, creamy layer and reserve the coconut water for drinks and shakes.

2. Make the crust: Pulse the cashews and almonds in a food processor until a nut meal begins to form. Then add the rest of the crust ingredients and pulse until completely combined.

3. Press the crust mixture into the bottom of a 10-inch tart pan and up the sides as much as possible. Place the pan in the fridge to harden the crust a bit.

4. While the crust is chilling, make the filling: In a medium saucepan over medium heat, whisk together the sunflower seed butter, honey, vanilla extract, cinnamon, and coconut cream until smooth and well combined. Once smooth, reduce the heat to low and add the gelatin ½ teaspoon at a time, whisking continuously, until the gelatin has completely dissolved and the mixture has thickened.

5. Pour the filling mixture over the crust and smooth it out with a spatula. Refrigerate for at least 3 hours, until firm.

6. Once the pie is firm, make the whipped cream.

7. Melt the chocolate in a double boiler or in a bowl in the microwave. Using a spoon, scoop up the melted chocolate and pour it over the pie, moving the spoon back and forth to create a pretty pattern. Pipe the whipped cream on top of the pie as desired and serve immediately.

8. Store the pie in the refrigerator, covered, for up to 1 week.

carrot cake layered
"cheesecake"

Yield: One 6-inch, two-layer cake (serving 10)

Prep time: 20 minutes, plus at least 3 hours to soak the cashews, at least 8 hours to chill the cake, and time to make the whipped cream

Cook time: 20 to 25 minutes

● ● ● ●

for the cheesecake layer:

1 cup raw cashews

½ cup raw macadamia nuts

½ cup honey

1 tablespoon lemon juice

¼ cup full-fat coconut milk

½ cup melted coconut oil

for the carrot cake:

1½ cups finely shredded carrots

1 cup blanched almond flour

3 large eggs

¼ cup melted butter, ghee, or coconut oil

⅓ cup maple syrup

1 tablespoon pumpkin pie spice

½ teaspoon baking soda

½ teaspoon baking powder

¼ teaspoon fine sea salt

for garnish:

1 batch Whipped Cream (page 296)

¼ cup chopped walnuts

I can't tell you the number of times I went to the Cheesecake Factory growing up. We would wait in the lobby for our table while pressing our faces against the windows that displayed the vast array of cheesecakes. I don't know why I'm saying "we"; *I'm an only child…it was only me pressing my face against the windows.* Anyhoo, their genius dessert marketing tactic always got me to order cheesecake at the end of the meal, no matter how full I was. It wasn't always worth it since I felt terrible afterward. But this cheesecake won't make you feel terrible, and it will be totally worth it. Bonus!

1. Soak the cashews and macadamia nuts in water for at least 3 hours, then drain and set aside.

2. Preheat the oven to 350°F. Grease two 6-inch springform pans.

3. Place all the ingredients for the carrot cake in a large bowl and mix well until smooth. Pour half of the batter into each springform pan. Bake for 20 to 25 minutes, until the cakes are cooked through and no longer jiggly in the middle. Let cool completely in the pans.

4. Place the soaked nuts in a food processor and puree until smooth and creamy. Add the honey, lemon juice, and coconut milk and puree until well combined. Add the melted coconut oil while the food processor is running. Let the cheesecake mixture puree for a few minutes—the longer, the better, so be patient. It should develop a very creamy texture.

5. Pour the cheesecake layer into one of the springform pans, on top of one of the carrot cakes, then smooth out the top. Place both pans in the refrigerator to chill overnight.

6. Remove the cakes from the pans. Stack the plain carrot cake on top of the cheesecake layer.

7. Make the whipped cream. Garnish the assembled cake with whipped cream and chopped walnuts. Slice with a warm knife, then let the cake sit for 5 to 10 minutes to come to room temperature before serving.

This cake changed my life. If you're like me (food-obsessed), you remember certain days when you tried certain foods, and those memories stay with you forever. I don't remember people's birthdays or presents that were given to me or even which pants I wore yesterday, but I remember the pie

my mom made and the sea bass I had in Vegas. Food memories stick with me. And this cake will stick with me forever. I absolutely, positively, 100 percent love this cake with every ounce of my soul.

layered flourless
chocolate cake

Yield: One 6-inch, two-layer cake
(serving 10)

Prep time: 20 minutes, plus time to
make the frosting

Cook time: 1 hour to 1 hour 15
minutes

1 cup dark chocolate chips

7 tablespoons butter

4 large eggs, separated

1 cup granulated maple sugar,
divided

1 tablespoon tapioca flour/starch

½ batch Vanilla Buttercream
Frosting (page 248)

½ batch Chocolate Buttercream
Frosting (page 248)

Tasty tip:
This cake doesn't even
need frosting. If you're not
in the mood to make it,
just sprinkle a little cocoa
powder on top, or top it
with whipped cream
(page 296).

Hayley is the reason this cake is so beautiful. *She loves frosting cakes as much as I love eating cakes.* So when I told her I wanted to ice the cake in some pretty way (meaning I wanted to throw icing on it in hopes of it looking "artsy"), she turned into cake-mode Hayley and created this masterpiece. Believe me, this cake doesn't need the frosting; it's delicious by itself. But if you want to wow your guests, all you need is a piping bag with a star tip. Google a video and master the art. It's crazy easy once you get it down!

1. Preheat the oven to 375°F. Grease two 6-inch springform pans. Line the bottom of each pan with a piece of parchment paper cut to fit the pan.

2. Melt the chocolate chips in a double boiler, then add the butter 1 tablespoon at a time until melted and smooth.

3. In a large bowl, beat the egg yolks with ½ cup of the maple sugar until thick and pale, about 3 to 5 minutes.

4. In another bowl, use a hand mixer to beat the egg whites to peaks. Scatter the remaining ½ cup of maple sugar over the beaten whites and beat to a stiff meringue, about 5 minutes. When you pull the mixer out, the egg whites should be stiff; that's how you know they're done.

5. Slowly mix the chocolate mixture into the egg yolk mixture. Use a large spatula to add a scoop of egg whites, then fold them into the chocolate mixture. Repeat this process, folding in the egg whites until completely combined. Add the tapioca flour and mix to combine.

6. Pour half of the batter into each springform pan. Drop each pan on the counter to remove any air bubbles. Place the pans on a baking sheet and bake for 1 hour to 1 hour 15 minutes, until the middles of the cakes are no longer jiggly.

7. Remove from the oven. Run a knife around the edge of each pan, then let the cakes sit until cool. They will sink down and the tops will crack. After 10 to 15 minutes, remove the cakes from the pans.

8. Once cool, place one of the cakes on a cake stand and spread the vanilla frosting on top. Then set the second cake on top and layer or pipe with the chocolate frosting.

samoa cupcakes

Yield: 7 or 8 cupcakes

Prep time: 10 minutes, plus time to make the frosting and caramel sauce

Cook time: 20 minutes

● ● ● ●

for the cupcakes:

1½ cups blanched almond flour

½ cup tapioca flour/starch

½ cup granulated maple sugar

½ teaspoon baking soda

½ teaspoon fine sea salt

2 large eggs, room temperature

½ cup melted coconut oil

1 teaspoon vanilla extract

for garnish:

⅓ cup unsweetened shredded coconut

1 cup dark chocolate chips

1 batch* Vanilla Buttercream Frosting (page 248)

½ batch Vanilla Bean Caramel Sauce (page 250)

* You may have frosting left over, depending on how much you use.

Believe it or not, I used to be a Girl Scout. You probably wouldn't guess it with my little sailor mouth (and I've kept it under control for this book), but I used to go door-to-door selling cookies. I was terrible at it; I guess I just don't have the sales gene. I'm pretty sure my parents bought most of my cookies to help support my troop. That meant that *a ton* of Samoa cookies were stocked in my household throughout the year. Those were by far the best cookies, right next to Thin Mints. These cupcakes are inspired by my 6-year-old Girl Scout, terrible salesperson self.

1. Preheat the oven to 350°F.

2. In a large bowl, mix together the flours, maple sugar, baking soda, and salt.

3. In a medium bowl, whisk together the eggs, coconut oil, and vanilla extract. Pour the wet ingredients into the dry ingredients and mix until well combined.

4. Use an ice cream scoop to scoop the batter into 7 or 8 lined muffin cups or silicone muffin cups. Bake for 20 minutes or until a toothpick inserted in the middle of a cupcake comes out clean.

5. While the cupcakes cool, spread the shredded coconut on a baking sheet. Place in the oven to toast for 10 to 12 minutes, until golden brown.

6. Once the cupcakes have cooled completely, melt the chocolate in a double boiler or in a bowl in the microwave. Dunk the top of each cupcake in the melted chocolate, lift to let the excess chocolate run off, and place on a baking sheet. Place in the refrigerator to cool and harden for about 10 minutes. (Save the leftover chocolate to drizzle on the top of the frosted cupcakes.)

7. Frost the cupcakes with the buttercream. Top each cupcake with about 1 tablespoon of toasted coconut, then use a spoon to drizzle on some melted chocolate and then some caramel sauce.

8. Store in the refrigerator for up to 1 week. For the best texture and flavor, let the cupcakes come to room temperature before eating.

vanilla buttercream
frosting

Yield: 1½ cups (enough to frost a 6-inch, two-layer cake or 1 dozen cupcakes)

Prep time: 15 minutes

Most of my college memories are loaded with crappy cocktails, dancing on bar tops, and sometimes studying. For me, food always had to be included in study time. Thankfully, I had friends who felt the same way. We would buy sugar cookie dough, chips, cookies, and frosting and then study away. *I remember nothing about anatomy class or chemistry lab, but I do remember the animal cookies that I dunked in frosting while skimming my homework.* I guess studying really did pay off, because here is my very own buttercream recipe: my bachelor's degree in health and exercise science, hard at work!

1 cup (2 sticks) unsalted butter, softened

1 teaspoon vanilla extract

1 tablespoon full-fat coconut milk

1 cup organic powdered sugar, divided

1. Place the softened butter in a stand mixer fitted with the flat beater attachment. Whip on high speed until fluffy, scraping down the sides every minute or so, about 5 to 7 minutes—the longer, the better.

2. Add the vanilla extract and coconut milk and beat for another 2 to 3 minutes, until fully combined.

3. Turn the mixer off, add 2 tablespoons of the powdered sugar, and then turn on the mixer and process to combine. Repeat until all the powdered sugar has been added and the frosting is thoroughly whipped.

4. If not using immediately, store in a closed container in the refrigerator for up to 1 week. For the best consistency, bring the buttercream to room temperature and rewhip it in a stand mixer before using.

Try this frosting on:

Variation: Chocolate Buttercream Frosting
After whipping the powdered sugar into the frosting in step 3, add unsweetened cocoa powder as you did the powdered sugar, 2 tablespoons at a time. After adding 4 tablespoons, taste the frosting to see if you want a deeper chocolate flavor, then add more cocoa powder (up to 8 tablespoons total) if desired.

Layered Flourless Chocolate Cake (page 242)

Samoa Cupcakes (page 246)

vanilla bean
caramel sauce

Yield: 1 cup
Prep time: 5 minutes
Cook time: 22 minutes

1 cup heavy cream or full-fat coconut milk

1 cup fine maple sugar

1 vanilla bean, split in half lengthwise, seeds removed with the back of a knife

1 teaspoon vanilla extract

¼ teaspoon coarse sea salt

Caramel seems so naughty. *Almost sexy.* It's one of those desserts that's so decadent and rich, eating one spoonful is enough but really isn't enough at the same time. Does that make any sense? Sorry, this caramel sauce just has me a bit hot and bothered.

1. In a small saucepan over medium heat, combine all the ingredients. Stir until completely combined.

2. Bring to a boil, then set a timer for 12 minutes, being sure not to let the mixture boil over. After 12 minutes, reduce the heat to low and simmer for 5 more minutes or until the caramel coats the back of a spoon.

3. Remove from the heat, let cool for 5 minutes, and then pour into a container. Serve immediately.

4. Store in the refrigerator for up to 2 weeks. Reheat the caramel sauce in a saucepan before serving.

Tasty tip:
If for some odd reason you don't know what to put this caramel sauce on, I'll help you out:

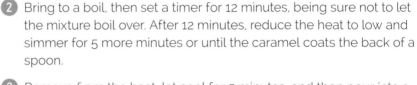

Blueberry Lemon Poppy Seed Ice Cream (page 228)

Samoa Cupcakes (page 246)

Caramel Apple Crisp (page 232)

Two-Toned Chewy Cookies (page 224)

The Fluffiest Mini Cinnamon Pancakes (page 48)

drinks & shakes

Time to cleanse the palate.

The first time I took a sip of beer in high school (lawbreaker right here), trying to be cool around other teenagers, I gagged. That obviously looked SUPER cool. I just couldn't do it; it tasted so bad. *To this day, I hate beer.* I'd rather have anything else. Water, lemonade, chocolate cake. Anything.

But when summer hits and my CrossFit gym is hotter than the asphalt outside because of our lack of air conditioning, *drinks are the only things that sound good.* Cooking is off-limits, baking is the worst idea in the world . . . so I just drink. Mostly protein shakes and iced coffees, but a mango margarita will sneak its way in there once in a while. I have always preferred eating my calories (in the form of chocolate) over drinking them, but sometimes only a cocktail will do the trick on a hot summer evening.

Whenever Paleo comes up, alcohol is always a touchy subject. If you're an alcohol person, *I don't want you to feel like you have to give up something you enjoy,* so I created some lightened-up drinks that you can make for yourself or for a party. Life is all about savoring the little things, and sometimes that means drinking your calories.

sweet almond
milk

Yield: 3 to 4 cups

Prep time: 5 minutes, plus at least 8 hours to soak the almonds and dates

If you go to the store to pick up a carton of almond milk, you'll likely find a long list of ingredients. And honestly, most of those things you don't want to be drinking. Making your own almond milk is not only cheaper and better for you, but it *tastes so much better!* Try making this milk with hazelnuts, pistachios, pecans, or even walnuts. Really, any nut will do. I just buy whatever is on sale.

1 cup raw almonds

6 Medjool dates, pitted

6 cups water, divided

½ teaspoon vanilla extract

10 drops stevia extract

1. Place the almonds, dates, and 3 cups of water in a closed container and refrigerate overnight.

2. Drain the water. Place the soaked nuts and dates in a blender along with the vanilla and stevia extracts, then add 3 cups of fresh water. Blend for about 1 minute, until smooth.

3. Pour the mixture into a nut milk bag or through 2 or 3 layers of cheesecloth set over a large bowl. Squeeze out the milk until no more remains.

4. Store the milk in a closed container in the refrigerator for up to 2 weeks. Shake well before using.

chocolate almond
milk

Yield: 3 to 4 cups

Prep time: 5 minutes, plus time to make the almond milk

At one point, I would drink chocolate milk every day after my work-out. But then I found myself dreaming about it while working out, before going to bed, and as soon as I woke up. *I was straight up addicted to chocolate milk* and had to cut the cord. This alternative has way less sugar, but it may be just as addictive. Just warning you now.

1 batch Sweet Almond Milk (opposite page)

¼ cup unsweetened cocoa powder

2 tablespoons honey or maple syrup

a few drops of stevia extract, if you prefer a sweeter chocolate milk

1. Place all the ingredients in a blender and process until smooth.

2. Store the milk in a closed container in the refrigerator for up to 2 weeks. Shake well before using.

chocolate hazelnut
iced mochas

Serves: 4

Prep time: 5 minutes, plus time to make the almond milk and hazelnut spread

I don't want you to think that just because you're eating Paleo, you can't have delicious-tasting drinks. *Nobody said that Paleo equals boring* black coffee. Try this iced mocha to mix up your morning caffeine routine. Hey, I rhymed!

1 cup chilled brewed coffee

2 cups Sweet Almond Milk (page 254), chilled, divided

2 heaping tablespoons Easy Chocolate Hazelnut Spread (page 292)

2 tablespoons unsweetened cocoa powder

1 drop stevia extract

1 to 2 cups ice

1. Place the coffee, 1 cup of the almond milk, hazelnut spread, cocoa powder, and stevia in a blender and process until well combined.

2. Divide the ice among 4 small drinking glasses, add equal amounts of the mocha mixture, and top each glass with ¼ cup of the remaining almond milk. Stir before serving.

salted caramel
mochas

Serves: 4

Prep time: 5 minutes, plus time to make the almond milk, caramel sauce, and whipped cream

This right here is a decadent treat. A treat that you should drink while snowed in, cuddled up in a blanket, *watching reruns of Sex and the City.* Why? Don't ask why. Just do it.

2 cups Sweet Almond Milk (page 254)

1 cup freshly brewed coffee

2 tablespoons Vanilla Bean Caramel Sauce (page 250), plus extra for garnish

2 tablespoons unsweetened cocoa powder

Whipped Cream (page 296), for garnish

1. Place the almond milk, coffee, caramel sauce, and cocoa powder in a medium saucepan and whisk to combine. Place the saucepan over medium heat and bring to a low boil, whisking every so often, about 5 minutes.

2. Pour the mocha mixture into 4 coffee mugs and garnish with whipped cream and extra caramel sauce.

pumpkin frappe

Serves: 2

Prep time: 3 minutes, plus time to make the almond milk and at least 8 hours to freeze

Personally, I think black coffee tastes terrible. It's bitter and has no pizzazz. I kind of see it like wine: It tastes awful, but I try to drink it because it's a grown-up thing to do. I usually drink only about a quarter of my cup of coffee before I get bored with it. But when I make blended coffee, ohhhhhh man, is that a different story! It's flavorful and delicious, and *I can act like an adult since I'm drinking coffee,* but still feel like a kid because it tastes so good. This frappe is really a win-win.

1½ cups cold brew coffee or strong brewed coffee

¼ cup pumpkin puree

¼ cup maple syrup

½ teaspoon vanilla extract

½ teaspoon pumpkin pie spice

2 to 3 cups Sweet Almond Milk (page 254)

1. Place all the ingredients except the almond milk in a blender and puree until smooth. Pour the mixture into an ice cube tray and freeze overnight.

2. Place the ice cubes in a blender with 2 cups of almond milk and blend until smooth. Add up to 1 cup more almond milk if needed to help blend the frappe. (You may have to do this in 2 batches to keep the blender from clogging.)

3. Serve immediately.

You may also like:

Chocolate Mint Green Smoothies (page 262)

Chocolate Hazelnut Iced Mochas (page 256)

Bloody Marys (page 264)

chunky monkey
breakfast shake

Serves: 1

Prep time: 3 minutes, plus at least 8 hours to freeze the banana and time to make the almond milk

1 banana, frozen

2 Medjool dates, pitted and roughly chopped

1 cup Sweet Almond Milk (page 254)

2 tablespoons sunflower seed butter

1 tablespoon maple syrup

1 tablespoon unsweetened cocoa powder

I make this shake all the time. I make it for a pre-workout drink, for a post-workout drink, for a snack, for breakfast, for another snack. It's been a constant in my life for the past year or so. Sometimes I add instant coffee and I'm even more hyper than I am in my natural state . . . which is a bit terrifying.

1 Place all the ingredients in a blender and process until completely combined, about 30 seconds.

2 Serve immediately.

Tasty tip:
Try adding some Raspberry-Strawberry Jam (page 294) for a little extra flavor!

You may also like:

Chocolate Hazelnut Pumpkin Bread (page 46)

"Peanut Butter" Cream Pie (page 236)

Dirty Chai Chocolate Muffins (page 38)

chocolate mint
green smoothies

Serves: 3

Prep time: 3 minutes, plus at least 8 hours to refrigerate the cans of coconut milk and time to make the almond milk

● ● ● ●

Green smoothies are very hip right now. Like, if your smoothie is green, you're just way healthier than everyone else. That's not the case with this smoothie. *This is more of a smoothie that you can hide vegetables in* to give to your kid who hates vegetables. Like I did.

2 (14-ounce) cans full-fat coconut milk, refrigerated overnight

1 cup Sweet Almond Milk (page 254)

1 tightly packed cup baby spinach

¼ tightly packed cup fresh mint leaves

¼ cup dark chocolate chips

1 tablespoon maple syrup

½ teaspoon peppermint extract

¼ teaspoon stevia extract

2 cups ice

① Refrigerate the cans of coconut milk overnight to help the coconut cream separate from the coconut water. When you're ready to make the smoothies, open the cans. The cream should have separated from the water and risen to the top. Scoop off the white, creamy layer for the smoothies and reserve the water for another use.

② Place the coconut cream and the rest of the ingredients in a blender and process for 30 seconds to 1 minute, until the smoothie mixture is light green in color.

③ Serve immediately.

Eat and drink more fresh herbs:

Guasacaca (page 286)

Chimichurri (page 284)

Basil, Mint, & Cucumber Gin & Tonic (page 267)

bloody marys

Serves: 4

Prep time: 10 minutes, plus 3 days to infuse the vodka (optional)

When I found out that I actually love a good Bloody Mary, I was floating in a boat on Lake Powell. A handful of the people on our 22-person trip hopped on the Malibu wakeboard boat to float while the sun came up. My friend Tyler brought pickle-infused vodka along with pickles, olives, peppers, salt, and pepper. Really everything you could think of, he had for these Bloody Marys. And *man*, were they outstanding. Infusing the vodka is a key component. And adding a million other ingredients so it feels like you're *having a whole meal in a drink.*

for the rims of the glasses:

1 lime

1 teaspoon lemon pepper

1 teaspoon smoked paprika

1 teaspoon fine sea salt

for the bloody mary mix:

6 cups tomato juice

½ cup tomato sauce

¼ cup pickle juice

3 tablespoons prepared hot horseradish

3 tablespoons hot sauce (I prefer Tessemae's or Frank's RedHot)

3 tablespoons coconut aminos

2 cloves garlic, grated

2 teaspoons celery salt

1 teaspoon smoked paprika

1 teaspoon fine sea salt

8 ounces grape or potato vodka (I used pickle-infused vodka; see tip)

for garnish:

cooked and peeled shrimp

green olives

celery sticks

pickle spears

1. Squeeze the lime juice into a shallow bowl. In another shallow bowl, whisk together the lemon pepper, paprika, and salt.

2. Dip the rims of four 16-ounce glasses into the lime juice, then into the spice mixture to coat. Then fill each glass with ice.

3. In a blender, blend together all the ingredients for the Bloody Mary mix, except the vodka, until well combined.

4. Pour 2 ounces of infused vodka into each glass, top with Bloody Mary mix, and then garnish as you please. Stir to combine before you drink up, buttercup!

Tasty tip: Try infusing your vodka with cucumber, jalapeño, rosemary, or even pickles, like I did for this recipe!

• To infuse your vodka with pickles, place ¾ cup vodka and ¼ cup pickle juice along with a couple pickle spears in a mason jar. Close and refrigerate for at least 3 days.

pomegranate
moscow mule

Serves: 1
Prep time: 1 minute

When people are kicking back with beers or cocktails, *I'm looking at the dessert menu instead.* To me, alcohol tastes terrible. Sure, you can cover it up to make it taste better, but I'd rather have chocolate. I understand that others enjoy alcohol, though, so I came up with this Moscow mule to make them happy while making myself happy as well . . . because I can't taste the alcohol in it!

6 ounces ginger beer
3 ounces pomegranate juice
1½ ounces potato or grape vodka
juice of ½ lime (about 1 tablespoon)
lime wedges, for garnish
pomegranate seeds, for garnish

1. In a glass, mix together the ginger beer, pomegranate juice, vodka, and lime juice.

2. Serve garnished with lime wedges and pomegranate seeds.

Tasty tip:
Make sure that the vodka you purchase is made from potatoes or grapes rather than grain.

basil, mint, & cucumber
gin & tonic

Serves: 1

Prep time: 2 minutes

Alcohol has never been my best friend. When I drink alcohol, my feet swell and get really hot. So I have to be aware of what shoes I am wearing while drinking. This refreshing gin and tonic makes the style sacrifice worth it.

½ large basil leaf

3 mint leaves

½ teaspoon granulated maple sugar

½ cup ice cubes

4 ounces tonic water

1½ ounces gin*

2 thin strips cucumber

slice of lime

1. In a glass, muddle together the basil, mint, and maple sugar until combined.

2. Add the ice cubes, tonic water, gin, and cucumber strips, and squeeze the lime juice into the glass. Mix and serve.

* Be careful with the gin that you purchase, because not all gins are gluten-free. My favorite gin is Hendrick's; it has never given me stomach issues.

frozen mango
margaritas

Serves: 2

Prep time: 5 minutes

I hate tequila. *Too many Mexico memories.* And I don't even like margaritas. But you know what? I really dig this one.

for the rims of the glasses:

2 tablespoons lime juice (about 1 lime)

coarse sea salt

for the margaritas:

1 cup frozen diced mango

¼ cup lime juice (about 2 limes)

4 ounces agave tequila

2 ounces Grand Marnier

lime wedges, for garnish

1. Place the 2 tablespoons of lime juice in one shallow bowl or plate and the salt in another. Press the rim of a glass in the lime juice, then in the salt to coat. Repeat with the second glass.

2. In a blender, blend together the mango, ¼ cup lime juice, tequila, and Grand Marnier until smooth, about 30 seconds.

3. Divide the frozen drink between the 2 glasses and serve garnished with lime wedges.

Try this cocktail with:

Mexican Meatloaf (page 106)

Pico de Gallo Salad (page 180)

Spicy Stuffed Plantains (page 110)

basics

Back to basics, but not too basic, fool!

Condiments were invented to make food more fun. To take food to another level. And when you begin eating Paleo, you lose a lot of fun condiments because you start reading the ingredient lists and find out that they're terrible for you. Or you find out that you could never win a spelling bee.

Well, I don't want you to miss out on the little things that make food way more interesting. We Paleo eaters should still have the opportunity to dip our Paleo pizza into Paleo ranch dressing. And if you are more of the pristine type, you should be able to eat your poached eggs with homemade hollandaise. *Everyone deserves to be healthy while enjoying every last bite.*

ranch dressing

Yield: 1 cup

Prep time: 5 minutes, plus time to make the mayo

● ● ● ●

I was very unhappy about being unable to have ranch dressing once I switched to Paleo. *Ranch was the only reason I ate salad.* Or French fries. Or pizza. Turns out, I liked ranch more than the actual food itself. Thankfully, my addiction to ranch has subsided, but my love for it has never passed. So if you need a Paleo pizza and a Paleo ranch dressing to pair with it, I gotcha covered. Life is just more fun that way.

1 batch Super Simple Mayonnaise (page 274)

½ cup full-fat coconut milk

2 tablespoons lemon juice

3 tablespoons minced fresh parsley

2 tablespoons minced fresh chives

1 tablespoon minced fresh dill

½ teaspoon garlic powder

pinch of fine sea salt and black pepper

1. Whisk together all the ingredients in a small bowl until well combined.

2. Store the dressing in a closed container in the refrigerator for up to 1 week.

Tasty tip:
If you prefer a thicker dressing, add half an avocado and the dressing to a blender and blend until smooth.

Try eating your ranch with:

The Perfect Pizza (page 136)

Pulled Pork Salad with Tomatillo Ranch Dressing (page 176)

Oven Parsnip Fries (page 184)

super simple
mayonnaise

Yield: 1 cup

Prep time: 1 to 2 minutes

● ● ● ●

This mayonnaise could not be any easier. It takes more time to get all your ingredients together than it does to actually make the mayo. *All you really need is 30 seconds,* and you have the perfect thick and creamy mayo!

1 large egg

1 teaspoon lemon juice

½ teaspoon Dijon mustard

⅛ teaspoon garlic powder

pinch of fine sea salt and black pepper

⅔ cup avocado oil

1. Combine the egg, lemon juice, mustard, garlic powder, and salt and pepper in a tall mason jar or cup. Blend the mixture with an immersion blender pushed to the bottom of the jar. With the blender running, slowly add the avocado oil 1 tablespoon at a time until the mixture begins to thicken. Continue blending until all the oil has been added.

2. Store the mayo in a sealed container in the refrigerator for 1 to 2 weeks.

Tip:
This can also be made in a food processor. While the food processor is running, slowly pour in the oil until the mayo thickens.

truffle aioli

Yield: ⅓ cup

Prep time: 5 minutes, plus time to make the mayo

● ● ● ●

Good Golly Miss Molly. Truffle aioli is a walk through flavor town. You can put it on burgers (page 112) or dip some parsnip fries (page 184) in it. Whatever suits your fancy.

⅓ cup Super Simple Mayonnaise (page 274)

2 teaspoons white truffle oil

1 clove garlic, minced

1 Mix all the ingredients together in a small bowl until well combined.

2 Store the aioli in a closed container in the refrigerator for up to 1 week.

hollandaise

Yield: ½ cup

Prep time: 5 minutes

Hollandaise really should be on everything. Steak? Yes. Sweet potatoes? Yes. Cake? Ew, don't be gross.

3 large egg yolks*

1 tablespoon lemon juice

½ teaspoon fine sea salt

dash of black pepper

dash of paprika

up to ½ cup melted butter or ghee

* Because the egg yolks are not cooked, be sure to buy organic, free-range eggs for the best quality.

1. Place the egg yolks, lemon juice, salt, pepper, and paprika in a blender and blend until well combined and smooth.

2. Turn the blender to medium-low speed. Slowly pour in the melted butter and let the hollandaise thicken to your preferred consistency. The less time you blend and the less butter you add, the thinner the hollandaise will be. If you prefer a thicker hollandaise, blend longer and keep adding melted butter.

3. Serve immediately. I recommend consuming this right away and not storing it for later use, since the consistency changes over time.

Try hollandaise on:

Breakfast Tacos (page 70)

Pulled Pork Benedict with Green Chile Hollandaise (page 74)

Spicy Sweet Potatoes (page 186)

bbq sauce

Yield: 1½ cups

Prep time: 5 minutes

Cook time: 10 minutes

Use this BBQ Sauce for Fall-Off-the-Bone Slow Cooker Baby Back Ribs (page 126).

2 cups ketchup*

½ cup water

2 tablespoons apple cider vinegar

1 teaspoon garlic powder

1 teaspoon onion powder

½ teaspoon chili powder

¼ teaspoon smoked paprika

¼ teaspoon black pepper

1. Place all the ingredients in a small saucepan over medium heat. Bring to a low boil, turn the heat down to low, and let simmer for about 10 minutes, until thick and reduced by one-third.

2. Store the sauce in a closed container in the refrigerator for up to 2 weeks.

* I use Sir Kensington's, Steve's Paleo Goods, or Tessemae's brand ketchup.

overnight slow cooker
caramelized onions

Serves: 6

Prep time: 10 minutes

Cook time: 10 hours

Sometimes making caramelized onions is too time-consuming. With this recipe, you can make them overnight or during the day while you're at work and BOOM, caramelized onions for days. *You're a busy person:* don't waste your time cooking onions on the stovetop! That's so last year.

5 large yellow onions, thinly sliced

¼ cup melted ghee or butter

2 teaspoons balsamic vinegar

½ teaspoon fine sea salt

1. Place the sliced onions in a slow cooker. Pour the ghee, balsamic vinegar, and salt over the onions and toss to coat.

2. Cover and cook on low for 8 hours. Then remove the lid, stir, and cook for 2 more hours without the lid on to help thicken the mixture.

3. Serve immediately or store in a closed container for up to 3 to 4 days.

Try these onions with:

Winter Squash Salad (page 172)

dairy-free pesto

Yield: ½ to 1 cup

Prep time: 5 minutes

● ● ● ●

1 cup pine nuts

1 packed cup basil leaves

2 tablespoons lemon juice

2 cloves garlic, roughly chopped

½ to 1 cup olive oil

fine sea salt and black pepper

Tasty tip:
Use other nuts to make your pesto: walnuts, pistachios, or even almonds.

Try these recipes in the book that use pesto:

Pesto is one of those sauces that is crazy flavorful and refreshing in a very small amount. Most store-bought pesto is filled with Parmesan. But with my pesto, you won't miss the Parmesan. *All you'll miss is when it's gone.*

1. Place the pine nuts, basil, lemon juice, and garlic in a food processor and pulse until the basil is broken.

2. With the food processor running, begin pouring in the olive oil. I like a thick pesto, so I use about ½ cup. If you want a more runny pesto, add more olive oil. Once it reaches your preferred consistency, add salt and pepper to taste.

3. Store the pesto in a closed container in the refrigerator for up to 1 week.

Pesto & Prosciutto Breakfast Pizza (page 64)

Pesto Shrimp & Rice Stuffed Peppers (page 158)

The Perfect Pizza (page 136)

hoisin sauce

Yield: ½ cup

Prep time: 5 minutes

Cook time: 10 minutes

I think my obsession for Chinese food started with hoisin sauce. Right after sesame chicken, rice, and fortune cookies. Hoisin sauce is sweet yet savory and *gives food so much flavor.*

½ cup coconut aminos

¼ cup sunflower seed butter

2 tablespoons molasses

1 tablespoon plus 1 teaspoon coconut vinegar or white vinegar

1 tablespoon plus 1 teaspoon sesame oil

1 tablespoon plus 1 teaspoon chili sauce

¼ teaspoon garlic powder

⅛ teaspoon black pepper

1. Place all the ingredients in a blender and puree until smooth.

2. Transfer the sauce to a medium sauté pan and simmer over medium-low heat until it has reduced and thickened, about 10 minutes.

3. Store the sauce in a closed container in the refrigerator for up to 1 week.

Try these recipes in the book that call for hoisin sauce:

Moo Shu Pork
(page 130)

Hoisin Salmon
(page 152)

chimichurri

Yield: ½ cup
Prep time: 5 minutes

● ● ● ●

1 packed cup fresh cilantro

1 packed cup fresh parsley

½ cup olive oil

¼ medium white onion, minced

juice of 1 lime (about 2 tablespoons)

½ teaspoon ground coriander

½ teaspoon ground cumin

½ teaspoon fine sea salt

Meat is just better with sauce. And chimichurri is one of those sauces that makes your *tongue do backflips.* Whatever that means. Chimichurri originated in Argentina but can be found in all kinds of restaurants, food trucks, and now your own kitchen. It is easy to make and can transform an ordinary meal into an extra-ordinary one. Have I gotten you jazzed up about this sauce yet?

1. Place all the ingredients in a food processor or blender and puree until smooth.

2. Store the sauce in a closed container in the refrigerator for up to 1 week.

Chimichurri goes on everything:

Parsnip Potato Hash Browns (page 60)

Oven Parsnip Fries (page 184)

Marinated Flank Steak with Chimichurri & Pomegranates (page 116)

Spicy Sweet Potatoes (page 186)

guasacaca

Yield: 1 cup

Prep time: 5 minutes

1 small white onion, roughly chopped

1 avocado

2 tablespoons white wine vinegar

2 cloves garlic, chopped

½ jalapeño, seeded and roughly chopped

2 packed cups fresh parsley

2 packed cups fresh cilantro

3 tablespoons olive oil

fine sea salt to taste

Think of this as a green salsa. Because that's pretty much what it is: a Venezuelan spin on guacamole and salsa. But together, in a happy, tasty, super flavorful mixture. *Once you make this sauce, you'll want to put it on everything.*

1. Place the onion, avocado, vinegar, garlic, and jalapeño in a food processor and puree until smooth.

2. Add the parsley, cilantro, olive oil, and salt and puree again until smooth. If the mixture is still chunky, add a bit more olive oil.

3. Store the sauce in a closed container in the refrigerator for up to 1 week.

Try guasacaca with:

Tostones (page 212) or Maduros (page 214)

Lechón Asado (page 138)

Carne Mechada (page 122)

Spicy Stuffed Plantains (page 110)

pizza crust

Yield: One 9 by 12-inch crust

Prep time: 5 minutes

Cook time: 10 to 12 minutes

3 large eggs

1 cup full-fat coconut milk

½ cup olive oil

3 cups tapioca flour/starch

¼ cup coconut flour

1 tablespoon baking powder

1 teaspoon fine sea salt

Lawd. This pizza crust. My saving grace. You can use it for pizza, or just make some breadsticks out of it! Genius, eh?

1. Preheat the oven to 350°F. Line a baking sheet with parchment paper.

2. In a medium bowl, whisk together the eggs, coconut milk, and olive oil.

3. In a large bowl, mix together the flours, baking powder, and salt. Pour the wet mixture into the dry mixture and whisk until smooth.

4. Pour the dough onto the lined baking sheet and use a silicone spatula to spread it out flat. The crust will puff up a bit as it bakes, so try to get it as flat as possible. Make the crust any shape you want it, but try to fill most of the baking sheet.

5. Bake for 10 to 12 minutes, until the crust is cooked through in the middle. It should feel like soft bread when you lightly press a finger in the center. Let cool for 5 minutes before adding toppings as desired.

Variation:

Individual Breakfast Pizza version (page 66): In step 4, divide the dough into 3 equal portions and form 3 smaller crusts.

Make some pizza!

Individual Breakfast
Pizzas (page 64)

The Perfect Pizza
(page 136)

tortillas

Yield: 1 dozen 4-inch tortillas

Prep time: 10 minutes

Cook time: 10 to 15 minutes

What is it about tortillas that makes a meal so much more satisfying? I don't know why we like to wrap meat in a little round, flat pancakes, but we do. And I'm definitely one of those kinds of people. And when I don't feel like making my own tortillas, I pick up some Must B Nutty almond flour tortillas online. You seriously have to try them; they are my favorite!

2 large eggs

1 cup full-fat coconut milk

1 tablespoon melted ghee, plus more ghee for greasing the pan

½ cup tapioca flour/starch

3 tablespoons coconut flour

½ teaspoon fine sea salt

¼ teaspoon garlic powder

1. Preheat the oven to 400°F. Line a baking sheet with parchment paper.

2. In a small bowl, whisk together the eggs, coconut milk, and melted ghee.

3. In a large bowl, whisk together the flours, salt, and garlic powder. Pour the wet mixture into the dry mixture and whisk until no lumps remain. The mixture should resemble pancake batter.

4. Place a large sauté pan over medium heat and add enough ghee to coat. Using a ladle, create a 4-inch tortilla (I usually cook two at a time). Cook for 1 minute per side, until slightly browned. Place the tortillas on the lined baking sheet and repeat until you've used up all the batter.

5. Bake the tortillas for 7 minutes, until they are slightly stiff.

Variations:

Tostada version (page 108): Bake the tortillas for 12 to 15 minutes, until toasted but not too crispy.

Moo Shu Pork version (page 130): Use only 2 tablespoons of coconut flour and create six or seven 6-inch tortillas.

Do you love tortillas as much as I do? Then try these recipes:

Breakfast Tacos
(page 70)

Street Fish Tacos
(page 148)

Slow Cooker Short
Rib Tostadas
(page 108)

Moo Shu Pork
(page 130)

easy chocolate
hazelnut spread

Yield: 1½ cups

Prep time: 15 minutes

Cook time: 10 to 12 minutes

Everyone loves Nutella. Everyone. This will be the *easiest chocolate hazelnut spread you've ever made,* so you can have it whenever you like!

1¼ cups hazelnuts

1 cup dark chocolate chips

1 Preheat the oven to 350°F.

2 Place the hazelnuts on a rimmed baking sheet and bake for 10 to 12 minutes, until the hazelnuts have darkened and the skins easily fall off. Remove from the oven and let cool for 5 minutes.

3 Use your fingers or a towel to remove the skins from the hazelnuts. They should come off pretty easily, but don't worry if there are some random pieces of skin that won't come off.

4 Place the hazelnuts in a high-speed blender such as a Blendtec, or in a food processor. Process for about 20 to 30 seconds, until completely creamy.*

5 Melt the chocolate in a double boiler or in a bowl in the microwave, then stir.

6 Pour the melted chocolate into the blender or food processor and pulse until completely combined and smooth, about 2 to 3 minutes.

7 Store in a closed container in the refrigerator for up to 2 weeks.

Add this spread to:

* If you're using a food processor, step 4 may take longer, because you will need to continuously scrape down the sides while processing. The hazelnuts also may not release as much oil as they're processed. If that happens, add 1 tablespoon of hazelnut oil at a time until you get your preferred texture.

Mini Chocolate Hazelnut Scones (page 44)

Chocolate Hazelnut Pumpkin Bread (page 46)

Chocolate Hazelnut Iced Mochas (page 256)

raspberry-strawberry jam

Yield: 1 cup

Prep time: 5 minutes

Cook time: 20 minutes

I love me some jam. When I was growing up, my mom canned the crap out of jam. She loved it. Because she made the BEST jam of all time. She would make so much strawberry jam that we would have it almost all year long. Back then, I spread it on bread almost every day. *Since bread and I are no longer friends,* I like to put jam in smoothies, in chocolate cups, and on banana bread. This jam makes me think about my mom and how lucky I am to have such a great jam-making woman in my life. Now go hug your mom! I'm getting all teary-eyed over here.

2 cups fresh raspberries

1 cup fresh strawberries, stems removed

½ cup honey

1 tablespoon lemon juice

1. In a medium saucepan over medium heat, cook the berries for about 5 minutes, until they begin to break down and fall apart.

2. Add the honey and lemon juice, reduce the heat to medium-low, and simmer for about 15 minutes, until the mixture has thickened. Then reduce the heat to low and simmer for 5 more minutes, until the jam coats the back of a spoon.

3. If you prefer a smoother jam, use an immersion blender to blend it to the desired texture. Store the jam in a closed container in the refrigerator for up to 2 weeks.

Try this jam with:

"Peanut Butter" & Jelly Cups (page 218)

Dirty Chai Chocolate Muffins (page 38)

Mini Chocolate Hazelnut Scones (page 44)

whipped cream

Yield: 1 cup

Prep time: 10 minutes, plus at least 8 hours to refrigerate the can of coconut milk

Have you ever seen that episode of *Family Guy* where Stewie talks about Cool Whhhip, emphasis on *whh*? No? *It's fine. It's not that funny.* I totally didn't almost cry from laughing so hard. Well, this whipped cream reminds me of Cool Whip. It's light and airy, sweet and delicious. You're gonna love it. Put this whhhipped cream on everything!

1 (14-ounce) can full-fat coconut milk, refrigerated overnight

4 tablespoons organic powdered sugar (for a whiter color) or fine maple sugar (for a light brown color)

½ teaspoon vanilla extract

1. Refrigerate the can of coconut milk overnight. When you're ready to make the whipped cream, open the can. The coconut cream should have separated from the water and risen to the top. Scoop off the white, creamy layer and place it in a metal bowl. Discard the coconut water or reserve it for shakes and smoothies.

2. Using a hand mixer, beat the coconut cream to smooth it out. Once smooth, add the powdered sugar 2 tablespoons at a time, beating continuously. Add the vanilla extract and beat until smooth.

3. Cover and place in the refrigerator for about 10 minutes to stiffen.

4. Transfer the chilled whipped cream to a piping bag and pipe it however you see fit on whatever you want! Store it in a closed container in the refrigerator for up to 1 week. To get the same texture after it has been stored, you will need to rewhip it.

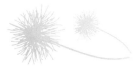

You'll love this whipped cream on:

Mini Cinnamon Pancake Bake (page 50)

"Peanut Butter" Cream Pie (page 236)

Salted Caramel Mochas (page 257)

recipe index

breakfast

Dirty Chai Chocolate Muffins (page 38)

Coconut Lavender Pistachio Mini Donuts (page 40)

Mini Chocolate Hazelnut Scones (page 44)

Chocolate Hazelnut Pumpkin Bread (page 46)

The Fluffiest Mini Cinnamon Pancakes (page 48)

Mini Cinnamon Pancake Bake (page 50)

Sweet Potato Waffles (page 54)

Blueberry Vanilla Chia Pudding Parfaits (page 56)

Breakfast Baked Sweet Potatoes (page 58)

Parsnip Potato Hash Browns (page 60)

Apple Fennel Breakfast Sausage (page 62)

Individual Breakfast Pizzas (page 64)

Prosciutto Herb Frittata (page 68)

Breakfast Tacos (page 70)

Pulled Pork Benedict with Green Chile Hollandaise (page 74)

poultry

Buffalo Chicken Casserole (page 80)

Sticky Sesame Teriyaki Chicken Wings (page 82)

Loaded Ranch Chicken Salad Wraps (page 86)

Coconut Cashew Chicken Fingers with Spicy Mango Dipping Sauce (page 88)

Super Simple Oven Chicken Fajitas (page 90)

Paella (page 92)

Chicken Carbonara Casserole (page 94)

Turkey Meatballs (page 96)

Honey Lemon Sticky Chicken (page 98)

Slow Cooker Jalapeño Popper Chicken Chili (page 100)

beef

Mexican Meatloaf (page 106)

Slow Cooker Short Rib
Tostadas (page 108)

Spicy Stuffed Plantains
(page 110)

Truffle Mushroom Burgers
(page 112)

Steak Frites with
Herb Roasted Garlic Butter (page 114)

Marinated Flank Steak
with Chimichurri &
Pomegranates (page 116)

Simple Beef Stir-Fry (page 118)

Rich & Hearty Bacon Beef Stew (page 120)

Carne Mechada (Venezuelan Beef)
(page 122)

pork and lamb

Falll-Off-the-Bone Slow Cooker Baby Back Ribs
(page 126)

Maple Bacon Pork Loin
(page 128)

Creamy Apple Sage
Brined Pork Chops
(page 132)

The Perfect Pizza (page 136)

Moo Shu Pork (page 130)

Lechón Asado
(Slow Cooker Cuban Pork)
(page 138)

Pineapple Sweet-and-Sour
Pork Meatball Skewers
(page 134)

Pork & Artichoke Stuffed Portabella Mushrooms
(page 140)

Lamb Curry (page 142)

Pistachio Rosemary
Lamb Chops (page 144)

fish and seafood

Street Fish Tacos (page 148)

Hoisin Salmon (page 152)

Mahi Mahi with Mango-Tomato Salsa (page 154)

Poblano Cream Shrimp Taquitos (page 156)

Pesto Shrimp & Rice Stuffed Peppers (page 158)

White Wine Butter Scallops (page 160)

soups, salads, and sides

Creamy Asparagus Soup (page 164)

Cream of Mushroom Soup (page 166)

Thai Butternut Squash Soup (page 170)

Winter Squash Salad (page 172)

Pulled Pork Salad with Tomatillo Ranch Dressing (page 176)

Pico de Gallo Salad (page 180)

Rosemary Bacon Brussels Sprouts & Apple Salad (page 182)

Oven Parsnip Fries (page 184)

Thai Coconut Chicken Salad (page 174)

Spicy Sweet Potatoes (page 186)

Honey Thyme Roasted Acorn Squash (page 188)

Lemon Truffle Roasted Cauliflower (page 190)

Rosemary Roasted Beets (page 192)

Crispy Smoked Paprika Radishes (page 194)

Oven-Roasted Fennel (page 196)

Sweet & Crunchy Green Beans (page 198)

Cauliflower Rice Five Ways (page 200)

Cauliflower Puree (page 202)

snacks

Bacon Buffalo Deviled Eggs (page 206)

Sweet & Spicy Sesame Almonds (page 208)

Maple Vanilla Candied Walnuts (page 210)

Tostones (Fried Green Plantains) (page 212)

Maduros (Fried Sweet Plantains) (page 214)

desserts

Coffee Caramel Chocolate Almond Bark (page 220)

Buckeyes (page 222)

Two-Toned Chewy Cookies (page 224)

"Peanut Butter" & Jelly Cups (page 218)

Blueberry Lemon Poppy Seed Ice Cream (page 228)

Caramel Apple Crisp (page 232)

"Peanut Butter" Cream Pie (page 236)

Carrot Cake Layered "Cheesecake" (page 240)

Layered Flourless Chocolate Cake (page 242)

Samoa Cupcakes (page 246)

Vanilla Buttercream Frosting (page 248)

Vanilla Bean Caramel Sauce (page 250)

drinks and shakes

Sweet Almond Milk
(page 254)

Chocolate Hazelnut
Iced Mochas (page 256)

Salted Caramel Mochas (page 257)

Chocolate Almond Milk
(page 255)

Chunky Monkey Breakfast
Shake (page 260)

Bloody Marys (page 264)

Pumpkin Frappe
(page 258)

Pomegranate Moscow
Mule (page 266)

Basil, Mint, & Cucumber
Gin & Tonic (page 267)

Chocolate Mint Green
Smoothies (page 262)

Frozen Mango Margaritas
(page 268)

basics

Ranch Dressing
(page 272)

Overnight Slow Cooker
Caramelized Onions
(page 279)

Super Simple Mayonnaise
(page 274)

Truffle Aioli (page 275)

Hollandaise (page 276)

Dairy-Free Pesto
(page 280)

BBQ Sauce (page 278)

Hoisin Sauce (page 282)

Chimichurri (page 284)

Guasacaca (page 286)

Pizza Crust (page 288)

Tortillas (page 290)

Easy Chocolate Hazelnut
Spread (page 292)

Raspberry-Strawberry Jam
(page 294)

Whipped Cream
(page 296)

index